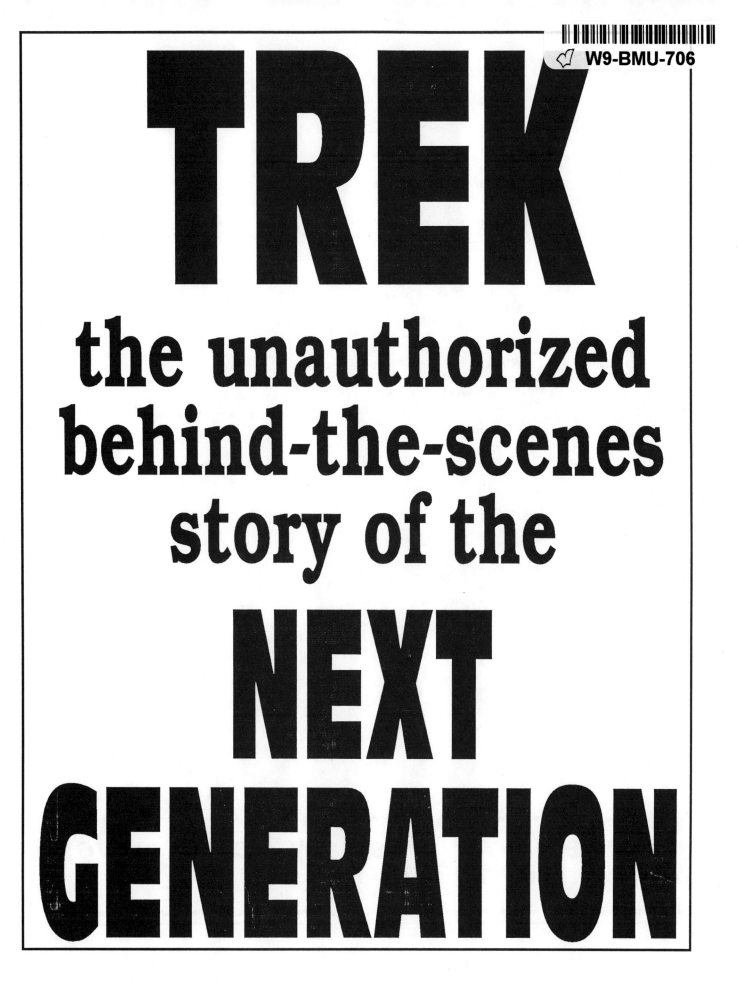

# TREK

## the unauthorized behind-the-scenes story of the

# NEXT GENERATION

# OTHER PIONEER BOOKS

•THE MAGICAL MICHAEL JACKSON
Edited by Hal Schuster. March, 1990. $9.95, ISBN#1-55698-235-6
•FISTS OF FURY: THE FILMS OF BRUCE LEE
Written by Edward Gross. March, 1990. $14.95, ISBN #1-55698-233-X
•WHO WAS THAT MASKED MAN?
Written by James Van Hise. March, 1990. $14.95, ISBN #1-55698-227-5
•PAUL McCARTNEY: 20 YEARS ON HIS OWN
Written by Edward Gross. February, 1990. $9.95, ISBN #1-55698-263-1
•THE DARK SHADOWS TRIBUTE BOOK
Written by Edward Gross and James Van Hise. February, 1990. $14.95, ISBN#1-55698-234-8
•THE UNOFFICIAL TALE OF BEAUTY AND THE BEAST, 2nd Edition
Written by Edward Gross. $14.95, 164 pages, ISBN #1-55698-261-5
•TREK: THE LOST YEARS
Written by Edward Gross. $12.95, 128 pages, ISBN #1-55698-220-8
•THE TREK ENCYCLOPEDIA
Written by John Peel. $19.95, 368 pages, ISBN#1-55698-205-4
•HOW TO DRAW ART FOR COMIC BOOKS
Written by James Van Hise. $14.95, 160 pages, ISBN#1-55698-254-2
•THE TREK CREW BOOK
Written by James Van Hise. $9.95, 112 pages, ISBN#1-55698-256-9
•THE OFFICIAL PHANTOM SUNDAYS
Written by Lee Falk. $14.95, 128 pages, ISBN#1-55698-250-X
•BLONDIE & DAGWOOD: AMERICA'S FAVORITE FAMILY
Written by Dean Young. $6.95, 132 pages, ISBN#1-55698-222-4
•THE DOCTOR AND THE ENTERPRISE
Written by Jean Airey. $9.95, 136 pages, ISBN#1-55698-218-6
•THE MAKING OF THE NEXT GENERATION
Written by Edward Gross. $14.95, 128 pages, ISBN#1-55698-219-4
•THE MANDRAKE SUNDAYS
Written by Lee Falk. $12.95, 104 pages, ISBN#1-55698-216-X
•BATMANIA
Written by James Van Hise. $14.95, 176 pages, ISBN#1-55698-252-6
•GUNSMOKE
Written by John Peel. $14.95, 204 pages, ISBN#1-55698-221-6
•ELVIS-THE MOVIES: THE MAGIC LIVES ON
Written by Hal Schuster. $14.95, ISBN#1-55698-223-2
•STILL ODD AFTER ALL THESE YEARS: ODD COUPLE COMPANION.
Written by Edward Gross. $12.95, 132 pages, ISBN#1-55698-224-0
•SECRET FILE: THE UNOFFICIAL MAKING OF A WISEGUY
Written by Edward Gross. $14.95, 164 pages, ISBN#1-55698-261-5

# Designed and Edited by Hal Schuster
## with assistance from David Lessnick

# TREK

## the unauthorized behind-the-scenes story of the

# NEXT GENERATION

## By James Van Hise

*Books for the entertainment buyer*

**PIONEER**

**Library of Congress Cataloging-in-Publication Data**
James Van Hise, 1949—
     Trek The Unauthorized Behind The Scenes Story Of The Next Generation

     1.     Trek The Unauthorized Behind The Scenes Story Of The Next Generation
(television)
 I. Title

Published by Pioneer Books, Inc., 5715 N. Balsam Rd., Las Vegas, NV, 89130.

First Printing, 1992

For Isaac Asimov—
the premiere science fiction writer of the 20th century, and one of the first STAR TREK fans.

**JAMES VAN HISE** writes about film, television and comic book history. He has written numerous books on these subjects, including BATMANIA, HORROR IN THE 80S, THE TREK CREW BOOK, STEPHEN KING & CLIVE BARKER: THE ILLUSTRATED GUIDE TO THE MASTERS OF THE MACABRE and HOW TO DRAW ART FOR COMIC BOOKS: LESSONS FROM THE MASTERS. He is the publisher of MIDNIGHT GRAFFITI, in which he has run previously unpublished stories by Stephen King and Harlan Ellison. Van Hise resides in San Diego along with his wife, horses and various other animals.

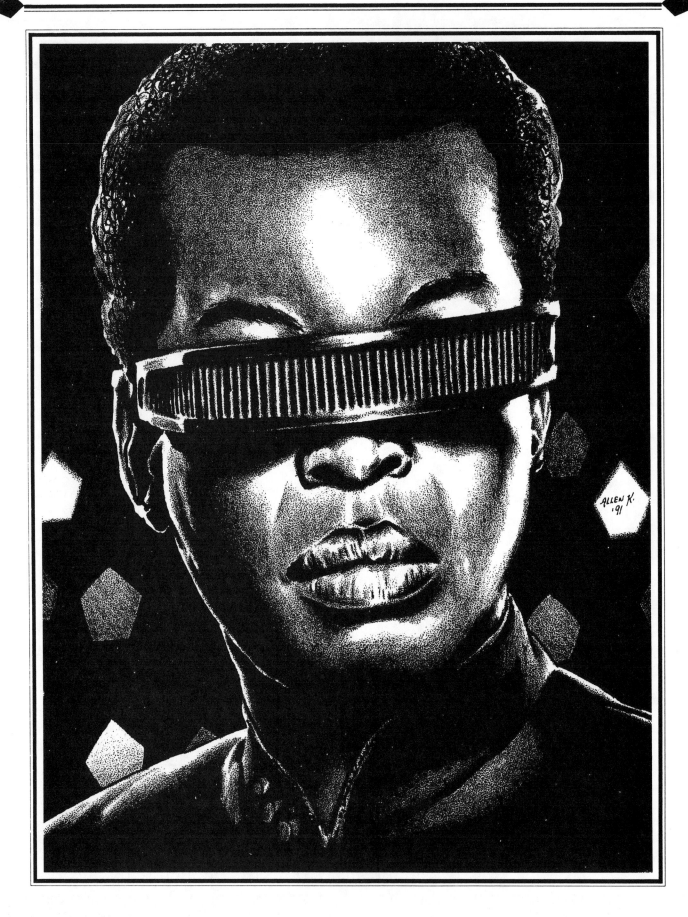

# BEHIND THE STORY

It's said that in Hollywood you have to get beneath the tinsel to get to the *real* tinsel. That's only a slight exaggeration. Creating a television series is a complicated process involving many people and a lot of compromises. While the credits for STAR TREK—THE NEXT GENERATION have always read "Created by Gene Roddenberry," not all of the ideas were his.

David Gerrold and Dorothy Fontana made considerable contributions in creating the show and Roddenberry's refusal to give them their due led to a falling out and ultimately a legal settlement. These and other controversies are chronicled in the lengthy behind-the-scenes overview of the first five years of THE NEXT GENERATION.

A lot of thought and design goes into the shows we see on TV. When it's a science fiction series like STAR TREK—THE NEXT GENERATION, the imagination is especially set loose. Not all of the ideas and stories make it to the screen and a number of these discarded plots are chronicled and examined in this book.

There are other sides to the creative process as well. For instance, were Guinan and Jean-Luc Picard actually inspired by real historical characters? In one chapter we examine that possibility. Also, the sometimes fine and sometimes distant line between real robotics and what Data is capable of is explored in a special chapter devoted to everyone's favorite android.

The Klingons were the black hat bad guys in the original STAR TREK, but in the new series we see many sides to their culture and personalities. Their growing importance in THE NEXT GENERATION is examined as well as how the Borg have changed and developed since they have become the new ultimate menace in the STAR TREK universe. Did you know that originally the threat of the Borg was meant to unite the Federation and the Romulans?

Finally, you'll get a sneak peak at the *third* STAR TREK television series: DEEP SPACE NINE. Will it really be as dark and disturbing as early reports have indicated? Did you know that Gene Roddenberry was involved in development sessions for the show months before he died?

Remember, there's a lot more to STAR TREK—THE NEXT GENERATION than what we see on the screen.

## —JAMES VAN HISE

ALLEN K. '91

# THE NEXT GENERATION:
# A Look Behind The Series

*When Paramount announced that they were bringing a new version of STAR TREK back to television on a regular basis, it seemed too good to be true. But it happened, and in defiance of some negative predictions (from people like William Shatner and Leonard Nimoy), the series has proven to be more than successful. But in many cases, this new show was just as difficult to bring to the screen as the original STAR TREK series was.*

**by T.S. Braxton**

# BEHIND THE SCENES: YEAR ONE

As mythologies develop, it sometimes becomes difficult to discern where the truth behind them lies. So it is with STAR TREK: THE NEXT GENERATION, now approaching its sixth season. The legend of STAR TREK is the legend of a man. Gene Roddenberry created something new (modeled after FORBIDDEN PLANET, which was itself based on Shakespeare's "The Tempest") and different and fought small minds endlessly in order to bring it life.

It died but was reborn, first in movies, then on television once more. But where did the impetus for THE NEXT GENERATION originate? It may be that the first desire for a new show, made less expensive by hiring a new cast, originated with Paramount, not with Roddenberry. After all, Roddenberry had not been struggling for two decades to create a sequel; the desire came when the executives felt that there was a market for it.

Still, there seemed to be no one around better suited to rev up a new STAR TREK series than the creator of the first one, so it was, ultimately, Gene Roddenberry who Paramount approached to create THE NEXT GENERATION.

Roddenberry's initial response to Paramount was negative: "I turned them down," said Roddenberry flat out. "I did not want to devote the tremendous amount of time necessary to producing another show. In order to keep the original show going, I practically had to disown my daughters. I had no time for them when they were in school; I didn't want to do that to my life again. . . there is only one way I know to write and produce, and that is to throw my energy at the project all the time. So when they began to think about a second series, I said I would not do it."

Paramount, by this time, was fairly adamant in their pursuit of Roddenberry, as Roddenberry himself related the tale: "[They] said, suppose we figure out a way that it could be done so that you would be in charge? I thought they were kidding! The studio said that I could be in full control of the creative standard; I asked a few questions, and they said, yeah, sure, you must know these things because you've been doing them anyway under network guidance. I told the studio that if they went the syndication route [that] I would go for it. Not only would I go for it, I would go for it full blast.

I told them I would find ways of doing STAR TREK that would give them extra elements. I think I have done that." And so, facing the challenge of what Leonard Nimoy would describe as trying to "catch lightning in a bottle twice," Gene Roddenberry set out to duplicate but transcend his accomplishment of the nineteen-sixties.

"Nothing's impossible, goddamit," he once insisted. "[The] most difficult aspect of [STAR TREK] was to go against all of that [negativity] and put a show together and believe you could do it, and collect people that could do it, and collect a cast that in its own way has the qualities of the old cast. It was the [seeming] impossibility of it that was the most difficult . . . "

Many other hands helped in the development of the new series; Gene Roddenberry was even seen as an impediment by some, and even he would eventually fade farther and farther into the background as a new generation of producers took charge, with his blessing, of his second great brainchild.

## THE FIRST SEASON

The first year of STAR TREK: THE NEXT GENERATION was a less than blissful situation for all persons involved.

Exits marked the first season. The actress portraying Dr. Crusher was unceremoniously canned at season's end, while another, Denise Crosby (Tasha Yar) cleared out somewhat earlier, allegedly at her own insistence, when her character was abruptly killed. But far more amazing was the considerable number of writers and other staff personnel who passed through STAR TREK: THE NEXT GENERATION during its first year.

Quickest to head on for different, even if less than green, pastures, were some who had done honorable duty on the original series. Old STAR TREK hand David Gerrold, hired on as a story editor along with Dorothy Fontana, cleared out in March 1987 with a number of complaints. Somewhat reticent about these to the public at the time, Gerrold maintained later that his departure was concerned primarily with unfulfilled promises, and unrelated to his failure to get a STAR TREK episode produced with a somewhat gay-themed story.

He did observe, however, that the high turnover rate involved in the inception of ST-TNG was not that common for new shows in Hollywood.

On the other hand, voices at Paramount alleged that Gerrold was abrasive and counter-productive during the start-up of the series, something flatly denied by Gerrold and by D. C. Fontana as well. (Fontana and Gerrold were among those who ultimately filed grievances with the Writer's Guild.)

In October of that year, Fontana, whose presence was intended as a vitally important link between the sixties show and its eighties offspring, also departed. She was unhappy with Roddenberry's tampering of her work. Fontana had been distressed by the fashion in which her original "Encounter at Farpoint" script had been grafted onto Roddenberry's cliched and fairly familiar "humanity-on-trial" plot. Ultimately, Fontana only contribute four scripts to the series, all rewritten extensively by Roddenberry.

## CREDIT WHERE CREDIT IS DUE

Both Dorothy Fontana and David Gerrold felt that they had contributed to the development of the series concept and didn't receive their due credit. (Eventually, a settlement was made with each of them, for an undisclosed amount, but the series would always be officially described as created by Gene Roddenberry.) Roddenberry certainly never admitted to any such contribution from Fontana or Gerrold; in fact, of Gerrold, he commented that "I had [Gerrold] on staff for many, many months, [and] he never wrote an episode we could shoot."

Of course, later Gerrold was vocal about ST-TNG failing to address sexual issues in a clear-headed, adult manner; as can be seen in the following description of two versions of the same unproduced script, even a low-key attempt to introduce gay characters to the STAR TREK universe would not sit well with Roddenberry or others.

For all of STAR TREK's high handed protestations of political correctness regarding a liberal, humanistic viewpoint , sexual politics, whether with regard to women or to sexual minorities, would be a blind spot for Roddenberry and his heirs on ST-TNG.

Gerrold's "Blood And Fire" involved the Enterprise in investigating a distress call from the Copernicus research vessel. An Away Team beams over to the Copernicus; it consists of Riker, Tasha, Geordi and three male characters named Freeman, Eakins and Hodel. (In an interesting note, this early NEXT GENERATION script features Worf as the Transporter Chief.) When the Away Team beams to the Copernicus, they encounter a sparkling cloud of the sort familiar on the old show, barely perceptible at first but quickly becoming more obvious.

As Hodel and Eakins try to reactivate a computer console, Hodel, obviously a busybody, muses on the relationship between Eakins and Freeman; they've been together for two years, ever since Starfleet Academy, says Eakins.

Life readings on the ship are weak, and the mummified body of a crew member, utterly devoid of blood, is found. A surviving crew member, hysterical, is also found, but he grabs a phaser and kills himself. As he disappears, more of the red and gold particles are seen. Meanwhile, Data's researches on the Enterprise have revealed that the strange particles are plasmasites, better known as Regulan bloodworms.

This is such a vile incurable disease that Starfleet forbids rescue attempts of anyone infected. An intense series of shocks ensues, as Hodel is attacked by the worms and Eakins must decide to kill the man in order to end his hellish torments. The rest of the Away Team is eventually beamed away to the Copernicus cargo bay, and quarantined inside a slowly weakening repulsor field along with a handful of Copernicus survivors including one Yarell. Yarell, apparently, was on a Federation-sanctioned investigation onto whether or not the bloodworms could be neutralized once they'd infested a human host.

Beverly Crusher beams over to the Copernicus over Picard's objections.

Some Enterprise personnel express fear that the contagion will spread to their ship, a sentiment quickly put in its place by Picard. Crusher, meanwhile, intends to remove everyone's blood and replace it with transfusions (!), a plan somewhat hampered by a shortage of artificial blood.

A blood drive is organized on the Enterprise. As the transfusions proceed, the Copernicus officers are beamed over to the Enterprise, where Picard suspects that the bloodworm research may have potential military misapplications.

Eventually, Riker, Eakins and Freeman are the last to go. With the repulsor field collapsing, Freeman forces the other two men to beam back to the Enterprise. The field collapses; sensors indicate that Freeman is still infected, and Freeman kills himself with a phaser blast.

Picard wants to destroy the Copernicus, but that might simply release the bloodworms into space. Then it is discovered that the Copernicus is on a course into Ferengi territory; Yarell, who has planned to destroy the Ferengi with the disease, pulls out a vial of bloodworms that he will release if

Picard interferes; Eakins pulls a phaser on Yarell; Yarell's subordinate, Blodgett, grabs the vial and swallows the bloodworms! He then takes an experimental cure devised by Dr. Crusher and is beamed back to the Copernicus, where Crusher's theory is proven correct and the bloodworms metamorphose into a beautiful, non lethal life form, with Blodgett sacrificing his life in the process.

This was Gerrold's commentary on AIDS. It certainly was no more heavy handed than other STAR TREK takes on current issues; it also was a pretty action-packed story. Gerrold's take on a Federation where everyone was equal and treated as such, regardless of anything, seems perfectly in keeping with the whole open-minded viewpoint of the series. Unfortunately, it didn't keep with current notions of marketability. Gerrold himself eventually made his drafts of "Blood and Fire" publicly available, and had a few words regarding it at a public appearance.

"What I wanted to do was deal with Regulan bloodworms," he explained, "because we had mentioned them in "The Trouble With Tribbles.""

People were always asking me about them, but who knows what a Regulan bloodworm is? At that particular time there was a lot in the news about the AIDS panic and people not donating blood; blood donorship was a major issue for me and always has been, and to hear that donorship was down because of fear of AIDS exposure, I wanted to do a story where at some point maybe everybody on the Enterprise must roll up their sleeves to donate blood to save the lives of some of their crew members. . . So that was floating around in my head. Also, we had a discussion of whether or not we could use Mike Minor as our art director. Unfortunately, Mike was very sick with AIDS at the time and has since passed away, which is a great loss to us."

Gerrold added, "In November of 1986, we all— Gene [Roddenberry] and I, George Takei, Robin Curtis and some others— were at a convention in Boston.

It was a twentieth anniversary celebration, and they had invited us all before they knew there was going to be a STAR TREK: THE NEXT GENERATION, so we all went out there and they were thrilled, because we were able to talk about what we planned to do on the new show, and they were very excited.

"There is apparently a gay science fiction club in Boston and they said, 'Gene, we've always had, on STAR TREK in the past, minorities clearly represented, isn't it time we had a gay crew member on the Enterprise ?

He said, 'You're probably right, sooner or later we'll have to address the issue and I'll have to give serious thought to it.' I thought, 'Okay, fine,' because I was sitting at the back taking notes. Whatever Gene said was going to be policy. We came back to Los Angeles and I'm still making notes for the bible and other things, and we're at a meeting with Eddie Milkis, Bob Justman, John D.F. Black, Gene and myself, and Gene said, 'We should probably have a gay character on STAR TREK. We seriously have to be willing to address the issue.' So I said, 'Okay, now I know [that] Gene seriously meant what he said in Boston, and I know that that's story material we could do.

"At that time I felt very positive, because by saying we could do that kind of story, Gene was also indicating a willingness to do a whole range of story material. As a writer I was excited, not just by that particular idea, but by the whole range of story ideas that were available. All of this [was] floating around in my head. I wanted to do a story that somehow acknowledged the AIDS fear, something about blood donorship.

I started blocking out a story called "Blood And Fire" about Regulan bloodworms. It started with the idea that we find a ship that has been infected, and if you have a starship that is infected, what do you do without bringing the infection to your ship? I thought we should make it [such] a really horrendous thing that there's a standing Starfleet order that when you run into a ship that's infected with bloodworms, the order is to destroy that ship immediately because, [a.], it is the merciful thing to do, and [b.], the last three ships that tried to save an infected population were also infected and died horribly.

"In the first few stories written, we saw that they were a little soft and there wasn't much action, and to balance that I wanted to do a show that had a lot of hard action and adventure in it. So the idea [was] that they could find another ship infected with the bloodworms and have a major problem, and to make it even more serious, first the Away Team beams over and then they find out [that] the ship is infected with bloodworms.

"That's where I started; then I worked out the life cycle of the bloodworms, that they grow in your blood until they reach a certain point and then, like malaria, they explode and start looking for new flesh. It was a very graphic kind of suggestion. I had a lot of fun with it, Dorothy [Fontana] liked it and Herb Wright loved it, saying that it was the kind of story we needed to do."

As for the scene suggesting a homosexual relationship between Freeman and Eakins, Gerrold stated: "I wrote that in a way to acknowledgethe contribution that gay people have made to the show and acknowledge they were all taking a large part of the burden for the AIDS epidemic, because this story was an AIDS allegory. Then we [dealt] with blood donation.

"When I finished ["Blood and Fire"] I felt that it represented some of the best writing I'd ever done for any television show anywhere, and I thought it could be a better episode than "The Trouble With Tribbles." Not as funny, [but] I wanted to do something distinctly different from "Trouble With Tribbles," and this is it.

I turned it in, and went off on the first STAR TREK cruise, and got a telegram from Gene that said 'Everyone loved your script, have a great cruise.' When I got back I found that the script was not going to be shot. I was told that Gene's lawyer [Leonard Maizlish] did not like the script and felt that this was not a good episode, and so on his advice, it seems, the script was canceled. That's what I was told by someone who was in a position to know. I don't have any proof in writing, so I have to qualify it by saying [that] someone told me. So, it was canceled for reasons that had nothing to do with its quality. It was just put on a shelf. I was very hurt and very upset about it, and the only way I can share it is to allow [the public] decide [. . .] if this would have been a good STAR TREK episode."

A second draft of "Blood and Fire," rewritten by Herb Wright and retitled "Blood and Ice," kept the basic adventure plot but dropped Gerrold's character material and the AIDS allegory as well; in this version, people who died of the bloodworm disease became zombies and chased the Enterprise Away Team around the Copernicus. It, too, was never filmed. (To show how early on this was, "Blood and Ice" also featured a Romulan as part of the Enterprise crew!).

## ABANDON SHIP

Besides the well publicized departures of D.C. Fontana and David Gerrold, there were other individuals who split the scene at or before the end of the first season of STAR TREK: THE NEXT GENERATION.

Eddie Milkis, a production supervisor with decades-old Trek links, finished up his obligation to do a single show but did not return. Another producer, Herbert Wright, defected to WAR OF THE WORLDS soon afterwards, as did various other production personnel, including Bob Lewin.

The role of story editor for the fledgling series was seldom held by any single person for long. Hannah Louise Shearer, who stepped into D.C. Fontana's shoes, Johnny Dawkins and Tracy Torme were among those who cycled their way through this seemingly untenable position. Shearer, like so many others, was somewhat vague about her reasons for leaving, although some have suggested that friction with Maurice Hurley, who was beginning to assume some of Gene Roddenberry's functions, was the underlying cause.

Reasons for these hasty departures varied from person to person, of course; Robert Justman, another 60's TREK survivor, left because he was simply ready to give it up and didn't feel as challenged by the show once it was underway. Apart from his writing efforts, Justman also served in a production role, considerably reduced once the season was underway, and was the man who cast Patrick Stewart and who hired young director Rob Bowman, who would ultimately prove to be one of the new show's greatest assets. Justman was partially replaced by then-production-manager David Livingston, who became a line producer and who would also direct such episodes as "Power Play" and "The Mind's Eye" in later seasons.

In one episode, "Code of Honor," Tasha Yar must fight another woman to the death over her no-good husband. Tracy Torme was offended by this particular episode's portrayal of a black planetary culture, which was redolent of 1930's African stereotypes.

The young Rob Bowman, who would eventually become STAR TREK—THE NEXT GENERATION's most prolific director, made his directorial debut with "Where No One Has Gone Before"— but was mistaken for a pizza deliverer when he came in for his initial interview!

## TOO MANY SUBPLOTS

Many see a major flaw of the first season in the excessive subplots that bogged down each episode, most of which were generated by Gene Roddenberry. Roddenberry had a tendency to go off on tangents from tangents, ad infinitum. In "Lonely Among Us," there was too much going on; Picard's brain invaded, alien ambassadors eating each other, everything resolved in a quick, neat pull of plot strings: it just didn't work.

Rob Bowman returned to direct "The Battle," a far from great episode but one of the first NEXT GENERATIONS to utilize different camera techniques. In order to emphasize the strangeness of Picard's experience returning to his old vessel the Stargazer, Bowman utilized a Steadicam, creating a different ambiance entirely than that used when portraying matters on board the Enterprise.

In an inexplicable piece of casting, Majel Barrett stormed the Enterprise as Deanna's mother Lwaxana in "Haven," an episode scripted by Tracy Torme from a spec script entitled "Love Beyond Time And Space" (submitted by Lan O'Kun). The cynical might suppose that Barrett's marriage to Gene Roddenberry might have had some part to play in her appearance on the show, but this is, of course, absurd and there is little to suggest that this connection had any bearing on Lwaxana's seemingly mandatory reappearance in each successive season of ST-TNG. Tracy Torme was actually rather pleased with her performance in "Haven," although he felt that the comedic aspects of his script were unnecessarily diluted by others.

The Dick Miller episode, better known as "The Big Goodbye," was more original than TV GUIDE gave it credit for; that magazine erroneously saw it as a swipe of "A Piece of the Action," when in fact the story had no relationship to the old STAR TREK episode.

Picard's alter ego, Dixon Hill, was originally dubbed Dixon Steele by writer Tracy Torme, after the Humphrey Bogart character in Nicholas Ray's IN A LONELY PLACE, but worried about problems with REMINGTON STEELE. The producers insisted on the change. The holodeck villain, Sirius Redblock, was portrayed without overt Sydney Greenstreetisms by Lawrence Tierney. Unfortunately, a scene in which Brent Spiner as Data waxes Hammetesque was trimmed due to time considerations.

"Datalore," in which Data meets his evil twin Lore, was originally slated to be directed by Joseph Scanlon. Scanlon didn't feel he could work with the script, so Rob Bowman was pulled from directing "The Big Goodbye" and wound up with "Datalore" instead. Bowman was unhappy with this switch. Never mind the fact that it would be Scanlon who got credit for the Peabody-award winning "Big Goodbye."

No one involved in the show even wanted to do the 'evil twin' episode! Still, Bowman did a creditable job of making a somewhat hackneyed story interesting. In fact, Bowman feels that the episode was a classic.

## DUPLICATE DATA

A duplicate Data also appeared, although somewhat differently, in the unproduced script entitled "Terminus." This script was revised by Robert Lewin and Dorothy Fontana from a submission by Philip and Eugene Price. Here, the Planet Bynax II is threatened by a strange alien device, but Data doesn't seem to find it threatening; he actually laughs at its passing.

The people of Bynax II have hidden beneath the surface, but they begin to return above ground when the situation is deemed safe, largely by Data's interpretation of the situation. An alien object identical to the one seen in space is found on the planet; the space version reappears and irradiates the planet with gamma rays, killing many of those humans who are on the surface at the time.

Data, feeling responsible, becomes suicidal, and seems intent on willing himself to 'die'! Data is confined to his quarters, but of course Wesley lets him out in response to an odd request to view the stars again. Data eludes him, and turns up on the surface, to be restrained by Riker, who has beamed down in the aftermath of the gamma-ray disaster. Data is beamed up and placed in quarters once more. News of this is announced on shipboard, awakening another Data, the real one, who returns to his quarters to meet his duplicate!

Eventually, it is determined that the two devices are only two of many which roam the universe, apparently helping humanoids, and creating the original Data along the way; but the destructive one was created to take revenge on a humanoid planet which maliciously destroyed one of the devices, only to go haywire (Nomad, anyone?) and now roams the galaxies destroying all and any humanoid life forms it encounters.

The benevolent device has been trying to rectify the situation and created the second Data to help matters. With the colonists safely underground, Picard beams down Data II along with a number of decoys devised by Wesley which will fool the evil device into thinking there are living humanoids there; the ruse works and the Enterprise nails the device with one photon torpedo. Data II stays on the colony to help rebuild, and the original Data apparently overcomes his psychological crisis and resumes his duty.

The destructive alien device in this clumsy script ultimately made its way to the television screen in "Arsenal of Freedom."

# THE WORST EPISODE

Writer Michael Rhodes ran afoul of Gene Roddenberry when he wanted conflict in a script he was working on. Roddenberry ruled out conflict as a dramatic device. This was the notorious "Angel One," easily one of the worst episodes ever of STAR TREK: THE NEXT GENERATION. Rhodes, who came to this one-shot STAR TREK: THE NEXT GENERATION assignment from scripting episodes of FAME, enjoyed working on the show, despite the disappointing quality of the episode as filmed.

Rhodes whimsically agrees that the show was sexist, and recalls how oblivious to this Roddenberry was. But then, Roddenberry in his 'politically correct' mode had always been oblivious to his own failings, especially in regard to the exploitation of women as sex objects in a vaguely adolescent, slyly leering manner.

When Rhodes suggested that the episode be used to examine the unconscious vestiges of sexism that might, perhaps, still linger even in the enlightened twenty-fourth century minds of Picard and his crew, Roddenberry dismissed the notion out of hand, and admonished a surprised Rhodes that there was no place for conflict in STAR TREK.

This was certainly an odd notion for an adventure show but perhaps a clear indicator of a certain muddled quality to Roddenberry's mental processes! Patrick Stewart observed that there was still considerable sexism in the scripts for STAR TREK: THE NEXT GENERATION, a fact that disturbed him. Eventually he and Jonathan Frakes protested, along with Marina Sirtis and others.

Rhodes, perplexed, couldn't quite fathom how to create an interesting drama without some sort of conflict. Still, his memories of working on the show, especially with the cast, are generally pleasant. There is no denying, however, that the creative process was undergoing some peculiar distortions during the first season of ST-TNG. No personal development, this is an adventure show— but please, no conflict, either.

Whatever the ultimate cause of the problems here, Roddenberry seems to have been at the center of things. By most accounts, the creator of STAR TREK was more than slightly possessive of his show, and allegedly was not interested in anybody else's creative input. Other viewpoints blame the problems on writers and producers striving to wrest some (or all?) control from Roddenberry.

## THE GUEST?

One episode, "Too Short A Season," was basically commandeered by its guest star, Clayton Rohner, who portrayed the aged, infirm ambassador Admiral Jameson. Although the episode was suppose to focus on that Rohner's character, the regular cast felt that Rohner didn't work in the ensemble manner too well. Director Bowman felt that the show was too verbose, more words than action.

In other words, boring. Admiral Jameson's state-of-the-art twenty-fourth century wheelchair was a problem, too. It cost the prop department ten thousand dollars but it didn't even move well enough to be anything more than a hindrance, and Bowman simply had to shoot around it. "Too Short A Season" was also the last episode of ST-TNG to bear a D.C. Fontana script credit.

Although scripted by Sandy Fries, "Coming of Age" was rewritten by Hannah Louise Shearer, and is perhaps notable as, first of all, the brief hope it raised that Wesley might leave the series, and, secondly, the lead-in to the forthcoming "Conspiracy" episode. Close on the heels of this came the superior "Heart of Glory," which kicked off the generally consistent STAR TREK: THE NEXT GENERATION trend of very good episodes involving Klingons, who, despite their semi-friendly status, still make for dramatic situations whenever they're around.

This marked Rob Bowman's last directorial outing during the first season. It also marked the first, and only time in which Michael Dorn's prosthetic Klingon teeth fell out, in a scene where he shows Wesley how a Klingon shouts. (Not in the episode as aired, unfortunately.)

Another ST-TNG staffer going AWOL early on in the game was producer/writer, Robert Lewin, who cited his interest in character development as his reason for leaving. Apparently, Roddenberry wanted an adventure show, and personal development was therefore out! For example, Lewin had meant for "Arsenal of Freedom" to develop the implied romantic relationship between Captain Picard and Dr. Crusher.

However, Roddenberry nixed the idea. The big emotional scene, with Picard and Crusher trapped in a cavern, was conveniently interrupted by a handy plot development before it could go beyond anything but the vaguest of hints. Originally, Crusher was going to reveal her true feelings to the gravely wounded Picard, but matters were switched so that Crusher was the injured party.

This change worked, but the failure of the scene to make its intended point was frustrating not only to Lewin but to director Les Landau and to most viewers. The scene was further marred by a fact not readily discernible to viewers watching at home; it seems that the sand in the cavern was infested with fleas, which made this shoot an utterly miserable experience for Patrick Stewart and Gates McFadden, who were under constant attack by the minute bloodthirsty creatures. Other sources have suggested that Lewin's departure may also have been stimulated by friction with Maurice Hurley.

Another weak point in the first season was the heavy handed manner in which current issues were inserted into the series. Like the unnervingly cheesy political commentary of STAR TREK's Vietnam-era "Omega Glory," "Symbiosis" ploddingly placed the drug controversy of the Twentieth Century smack (no pun intended) dab in the middle of the Twenty-fourth Century, when apparently, the only surviving thoughts on the subject came from the mind of Nancy Reagan.

DeQuincey, Coleridge, Huxley, Burroughs, Leary and other writers on the subject, whatever the rightness or wrongness of their viewpoints, seem to have had no works survive to Picard's time. Perhaps a significant part of the human literature did not survive, screened out for political correctness by the watchful eye of Gene Roddenberry.

To further complicate matters, the script for "Symbiosis" wasn't even finished when one-shot director Winn Philips came on board. This was to be a major bone of contention for much of the cast, regulars and guests alike; their characters positions seemed vague and unformed. The guest stars, including WRATH OF

KHAN veterans Merritt Butrick and Judson Scott, were cast using dialogue culled from an earlier episode! To make matters worse, "Symbiosis" was essentially a 'talking heads' show, during which various characters, primarily Jean-Luc Picard and Beverly Crusher, spouted off their own overblown opinions without moving around or doing much else of anything.

Beyond all this, "Symbiosis," although aired before "Skin of Evil," was shot after that episode, and was therefore the last episode shot with Denise Crosby as Tasha Yar (at least until "Yesterday's Enterprise"). Director Phelps, who would go on to direct a record number of L.A. LAW episodes (and to net an Emmy in the process), arranged a special parting tribute for Crosby: in one shot, well in the background, she waves goodbye to the camera.

## THE ATTORNEY/WRITER

Part of the problem with the entire first season (alleged in some of the Writer's Guild complaints about the show) was the notion that Leonard Maizlish, Gene Roddenberry's attorney, actually rewrote scripts—a violation of Guild priorities if ever there was one—much to the detriment of many writers' original visions. Officially, of course, Roddenberry himself did considerable rewriting on many, if not all, of ST-TNG's first-season scripts, which many feel was, in itself, a primary failing of the show's first year off the ground.

According to one source, Maizlish was the one who came up with the dismal manner in which Tasha Yar made her exit (although it was apparently Denise Crosby's wish to leave the show anyway). Maizlish seems, perhaps, to have served as an "enforcer" for Roddenberry, apparently making certain that Roddenberry's story idea, of death happening as a matter of course during a dangerous mission despite the different views held by the various writers involved in the "Skin of Evil" episode (originally scripted by Joseph Stephano).

There was considerable controversy among the show's staff regarding this death: some felt that it was cynically manipulative, while others felt that it made sense to avoid sentimentality (although the episode's end didn't avoid it at all). Still, Maizlish or no Maizlish, "Skin of Evil" will always stand as the STAR TREK episode where, at least for once, it wasn't the anonymous, red-shirted crew member we've never seen before who gets wasted by the episode's villain.

Most involved with the show felt that "Skin of Evil" was an unmitigated disaster; not only did they have problems making an oil slick a believable character, but they felt that the death of Tasha Yar was somehow a low point in the evolution of ST-TNG.

Writers Deborah Dean Davis and Hannah Louise Shearer wanted to create a romantic mood in "We'll Always Have Paris," and succeeded somewhat, but their original script's insistence that Picard do "the wild thing" some time in the course of the episode (discreetly, while a commercial was on, of course) was vetoed by a number of men involved in the production— most notably Patrick Stewart. The good Captain's chastity would remain firmly unviolated until the third season's "Captain's Holiday."

## BETTER SHOWS

One of the better first season episodes was "Conspiracy," which went all out with its exploding-head sequence and gratuitous grub-eating; this was a pretty intense one, but for some reason its paranoid conclusion never led to a sequel, perhaps because the Borg would eventually make a better threat than bugs from beyond the stars.

Writer Tracy Torme, adapting a story by Robert Sabaroff to THE NEXT GENERATION, had hoped to make "Conspiracy" a commentary on the Iran/Contra Affair, but this potentially controversial notion was nixed. A plot by Starfleet officers out to undermine the Prime Directive (already introduced six episodes before in "Coming of Age"), turns out to be the result of an infestation of alien insects, not part of Torme's original approach.

There was just no way he could get away with suggesting that the Federation was anything less than a perfect government. Retained were the dubious ending and the explicit violence, although Torme was not behind the exploding head at the end of the episode, which was put in by the producers.

In fact, the whole idea of the episode, its violence, and its unresolved ending caused quite a stir, but Robert Justman, Rick Berman and Bob Lewin backed Torme against the objections of Maurice Hurley, and the show stood pretty much as he had intended it, with the topical references subtly shoved under the carpet. Things would not go so well for writer Torme in the future; he would be left with the feeling that, as far a creative freedom for writers, the second half of THE NEXT GENERATION's second season was the best part of the series as a whole.

Coming close on the heels of "Conspiracy," the last episode of the first season, "The Neutral Zone," was a fairly weak examination of three cryogenically frozen 20th Century humans who find themselves awakened in the 24th Century; after a season in which the Ferengi devolved from would-be villains to comic relief, the series reintroduced those pesky Romulans (apparently incommunicado for seventy-plus years), although their ominously intended "We're back" seemed fairly anticlimactic.

Producer/writer Maurice Hurley had something more in mind with this episode: those strange attacks the Romulan complained about in "The Neutral Zone" would dangle as an unresolved plot device for quite some time. . . but there was a plan, as Hurley had meant for this episode to comprise part of a trilogy. It would have to wait, though. (Hurley, in fact, was a rare bird in the ST-TNG universe; he stuck with the show despite Roddenberry problems. His rewrite of "Where No One Has Gone Before" was axed by the Great Bird of the Galaxy, but Hurley, despite disappointment, did not abandon ship. A former producer for THE EQUALIZER and MIAMI VICE, Hurley was attracted to the challenge of a new kind of series, and was willing to accept certain restrictions in order to get ahead.)

An unproduced, alternative Romulan story, also featuring aspects that would make their way into "To Short A Season," was entitled, oddly enough, "The Neutral Zone." Scripted by Greg Strangis, it would have certainly made for a much better episode, especially as a season finale, than the completely different storyline which ultimately was to bear the same title.

In Strangis' "The Neutral Zone," a famous Starfleet security expert named Billings comes on board the Enterprise; Billings in confined to a wheelchair and is clearly a distant, lonely figure. He is also the man who led the mission which rescued Tasha Yar from her brutal home world, but he is completely oblivious to Tasha's efforts to better make his acquaintance.

Billings' mission is revealed in short order: the Enterprise is to take part in a trade negotiation which will involve, for the first time, the Romulan Empire; Picard's mission is to get the Romulan delegates there, and Billings is on hand to assure that all goes well.

To implement this, he compiles a list of all Enterprise personnel who have had contact with Romulans, and orders that they be dropped off at a Starbase for the duration of this sensitive mission. Ironically, this group includes inveterate Romulan-hater Worf, who Picard defends; Worf manages to remain on board, where he becomes involved in the obligatory Wesley subplot. Meanwhile, Beverly proposes an operation involving fluid drawn from Data's spine (?!?) to help Billings but Billings brusquely declines.

Romulan commander Gar, obviously against the accord he's been assigned to promote, beams aboard and dissension ensues. Matters grows complicated when the Transporter malfunctions while the rest of the Romulan delegates are beaming over; after some tense moments, they are safely returned to their own ship, but Gar is less than pleased, especially when data discovers a sabotaging device inside the Transporter controls console.

Unfortunately for Wesley and Worf, their separate subplot took them, without authorization, into the Transporter area; this does not bode well for them until Tasha turns up some security tapes (?) showing Gar inserting the device. The Romulan remains insouciant, claiming that the negotiations were leading to disaster anyway and that his actions were merely getting the problem out of the way quicker.

With all this sorted out, Billings consents to Dr. Crusher's proposed operation, and is able to walk. This is a rather uneven storyline but with a minimum of polish it would have been vastly superior to the different "Neutral Zone." It is interesting to note that a passing reference by Picard to an engagement with a Romulan ship sometime in his career is inconsistent with the history of Romulan isolation as described in the actual first-season finale. Writer Greg Strangis later became a producer of Paramount's short-lived WAR OF THE WORLDS syndicated science fiction series.

# BEHIND THE SCENES: YEAR TWO

By the end of the first season, it was apparent that some improvement was still needed. ST-TNG had apparently gotten off the ground, but, at an average cost of one and a third million dollars per episode, Paramount was basically throwing money away, at least in the short term. National advertising sales still left an annual deficit of nearly eight million dollars.

Of course, Paramount had a long-term plan, for they had learned from the original STAR TREK that the real money was in syndication. As soon as they could strip the show (run it at least five days a week in syndicated reruns), STAR TREK: THE NEXT GENERATION would become the money making machine Paramount dreamed of. They were willing to keep the show going long enough to produce a sufficient number of episodes to make such a syndication scheme possible. And of course, it ultimately worked, for STAR TREK: THE NEXT GENERATION would be in daily reruns nationwide by the end of the third season.

Part of the success of the show, of course, derived from the actors who brought THE NEXT GENERATION's cast to vivid life.

## A QUICK LOOK AT THE CHARACTERS

In the pivotal role of Captain Picard, there was the British stage actor Patrick Stewart, who had also been in such genre films as EXCALIBUR, LIFE FORCE and David Lynch's DUNE, the film which brought him to the attention of Roddenberry's production team. Stewart, much touted as a Shakespearean actors by the NEXT GENERATION publicity machine, was himself later to point out that in the stratified world of the classical theater he was generally classified as a "low comic," unlikely to land leading or even major supporting dramatic roles such as Hamlet or Othello.

It would in fact be television that would make him into a heroic leading man. But the man allegedly referred to as "Baldilocks" by his fellow actors has a reputation for difficulty, and supposed walks off shoots on a variety of pretexts. To top this off, a talk show appearance by an arrogant Patrick Stewart accomplished the extraordinary feat of making another guest on the show, a certain William Shatner, appear modest and self-effacing.

Whatever these failings, Stewart proved to be utterly convincing on screen as the dignified center of authority on board the Enterprise; his presence was always felt even when he occupied merely the background in any particular scene.

Picard's second-in-command, William Riker, was played by Jonathan Frakes, whose character didn't quite gel in the first season but would become more substantial and better-defined during the second year of shooting; David Gerrold is generally credited with the quite-sensible notion of having the second-in-command beam down to other planets, leaving the valuable head honcho safe on board.

British actress Marina Sirtis, as ship's counselor Deana Troi, successfully created a vague, new accent for her Betazoid character, which retained traces of her native accent but has about it a touch of "somewhere else." When out of character, however, Sirtis is quite obviously a Brit through and through!

Named after a STAR TREK fan who died after years of suffering from the disease cerebral palsy, Geordie LaForge, the ship's handicapped character (something Roddenberry had been determined to address) was ably played by LeVar Burton, most famous for his role in the miniseries ROOTS, but this character to would take some time to come into his own.

Most annoying, of course, would be Will Wheaton as Wesley Crusher, boy wonder. Roddenberry's middle name was Wesley, but his reasons for naming this vexing character after himself are best left unexamined.

Faring much better as Wesley's mother was actress/dancer Gates McFadden, who portrayed ship's doctor Beverly Crusher as a warm and dedicated person, but who was unceremoniously dropped at the end of the season by Gene Roddenberry: the Great Bird of the Galaxy actually went so far as to release a statement demanding that fans not write to complain about McFadden's departure, as his decision was final and irreversible. (Oh, really, Gene?)

## THE WRITER'S STRIKE

The primary problem encountered by STAR TREK: THE NEXT GENERATION in its second season was a sticky one: a strike by the Writer's Guild. To slide around this obstacle, Paramount dug out "The Child," a script written for the abortive TV STAR TREK II revival of a decade earlier, and reworked it to feature Deanna Troi as the lead character (originally Ilia). (Lost in the shuffle was Maurice Hurley's proposed sequel to "The Neutral Zone," in which he had hoped to introduce a new threat, the Borg, who would prompt an alliance between the Romulans and the Federation.)

Early in the episode we learn that Dr. Beverly Crusher has moved on up to bigger and better things, and that a new doctor is taking her place on the Enterprise. Doctor Crusher's replacement, Dr. Pulaski, was ably played by Trek veteran (and future L.A. LAW casualty) Diana Muldaur. But the character, although a welcome attempt to interject some much-needed sandpaper between the interpersonal relationships on board the Enterprise (especially where Data was concerned), never really quite cut it.

Tracy Torme has pointed out that Pulaski's abrasiveness was toned down almost immediately when the producers got cold feet and decided to make the character a bit more accessible rather than risk alienating viewers. And perhaps there was something all-too-familiar about this ship's doctor: old-fashioned, cranky, opinionated, and profoundly disinclined to use the Transporter.

Dr. Pulaski was Leonard "Bones" McCoy in drag, an ill-conceived attempt to re-create the old McCoy/Spock interaction with her and Data. Of course, Data, despite many similarities, is not Spock. (Even more than Leonard Nimoy isn't.) Thankfully, Pulaski faded out with the end of the season, and Crusher was to return, without even a word of explanation.

Also joining the cast of ST-TNG was a performer who had already achieved fame elsewhere: Whoopi Goldberg. Long a fan of the original series (Nichelle Nichols was her childhood inspiration), Goldberg actively sought a role on the series, and eventually became Guinan, the bartender.

In an interesting alteration which has by now become commonplace, Jonathan Frakes had grown a beard during the summer break, which fit the character of Riker well; some viewers even see the beard as an indicator of the improvement of the second season over the first, and tune out reruns with a clean-shaven Riker.

With all this going on in the first of the season, director Rob Bowman had his hands full, but he pulled it all together, with the help of a fine performance from Marina Sirtis.

In a first draft outline of a proposed script by Lee Maddux entitled "The Bonding" (dated October 9, 1987), the Enterprise again encountered a rapidly-maturing child. In this unproduced script, the Enterprise is called away from an important diplomatic mission in order to offer medical assistance to a planet undergoing violent social disturbances.

Apparently, the ruling class of Croton has strong telekinetic powers which allow them to keep their subjects satisfied. The revolt seems inexplicable. The problem lies in the fact that the laws of Croton have outlawed emotion. Matters come to a head when an elite Croton woman disguised as a commoner brings a baby on board, and dies, somehow placing the baby in the care of the ship's computer!

The child, Pattrue, grows much as does Deanna's son in "The Child," but is 'tainted,' from his culture's viewpoint, by his exposure to human emotion, especially once he becomes pals with Wesley Crusher. In a laughable wrap-up of the problem, Pattrue uses his mental powers to go through all the laws of his planet in a matter of minutes, finding, in the process, a means of invalidating the anti-emotion laws! He then returns to his planet in order to institute a kindler, gentler world order!

Not only does this bear certain superficial resemblances to "The Child," it also features a subplot, later used in the series in "The Icarus Factor," in which Wesley and others help an out-of-sorts Worf to re-enact an important Klingon initiation ritual.

Writer Robert Iscove faced some problems with the Riker father/son conflict in "The Icarus Factor," as one of Roddenberry's laws deems that such feelings have been outgrown by humans by the twenty-fourth century.

On the writing front, Tracy Torme, who had penned such popular first season episodes as "Haven," "The Big Goodbye," and "Conspiracy," was given the title of 'creative consultant', but would find in time that a new title doesn't always bring new freedoms from control.

Rob Bowman finally got to direct a holodeck/period piece episode with "Elementary Dear Data," in which a holodeck-generated Moriarity (Daniel Davis), designed, in a slip of Geordi's tongue, to be a match for Data rather than for Sherlock Holmes, manages to take over the ship from the holodeck.

In the original script, when Moriarity sends a drawing of the Enterprise from the holodeck to the bridge, Picard realizes that Moriarity can leave the holodeck, too, and actually lies to Moriarity in order to trick him. This is explicit in the original version; Data actually comments on the Captain's prevarication.

Gene Roddenberry would have none of it. No one else had a problem with it. In the context, it was probably Picard's only way out of losing control of his ship. But, at Roddenberry's insistence, the ending of the story was emasculated.

Bowman got the royal run-around from the front office on this one; originally intended as an eight-day shoot, they cut it back to seven over the protests of Bowman, who felt that nine days were really needed. (The London set cost 125 thousand dollars, which didn't sit too well with the accountants.) Still, within these restrictions, it was a superb episode; largely thanks to Bowman, it was already apparent that the second season of ST-TNG was going to be better than the first.

Writer Tracy Torme openly acknowledges borrowing the title of "The Schizoid Man" from an episode of THE PRISONER. (That episode of THE PRISONER had Patrick MacGoohan facing an exact duplicate of himself, prompting the momentary suspicion that this NEXT GENERATION episode might be another Data-meets-Lore episode, but this was not to be.)

The story finds Data befriending the dying Ira Graves, who returns the favor by transferring his mind into Data's body. Despite a quick solution to the crisis, this was another good Brent Spiner showcase. It had been intended as a more humorous Data vehicle by Tracy Torme, but the humor was trimmed considerably by the producers to avoid another "Outrageous Okona."

This was much better, but Torme had originally gotten more mileage out of Data's temporary beard in an attempt to more fully exploit the ego theme of the show. In fact, Torme's final scene, as first scribed, would have had an annoyed Picard discussing Data's altered appearance with Riker on the bridge; the expectation intended was that Data had reapplied his beard, but the punch line would have been that he'd actually cut off all his hair.

"The Schizoid Man" also introduced, but only for one episode, an new Vulcan character, Dr. Solar, played by Suzy Plakson. Tracy Torme had hoped to have a romance develop between Solar and Worf, but the producers had something else in mind, a half-Klingon woman. Torme felt that his idea would have been more interesting. Perhaps so, but K'Ehleyr, when she turned up in "The Emissary," would prove to be a good character, and one who certainly bore a strong resemblance to Solar, since she would also be played by Suzy Plakson.

Another classic Klingon episode, "A Matter of Honor" (directed by Rob Bowman) finds Riker as an exchange officer on a Klingon ship, which gave Jonathan Frakes a chance to be something other than Mister Nice Guy. Bowman once described the episode as a 'male bonding' ritual, as he and Frakes both used the story as a chance to work off steam generated by their respective marital difficulties. (Bowman was going through a divorce at the time.) Bowman also 'invented' a Klingon ladder by appropriating a bicycle rack from the studio lot and mounting it sideways!

# A STAR IS BORN

Nominated as best original script for a dramatic series that year, Melinda Snodgrass' script for "The Measure of a Man" also landed her a job as a story editor for ST-TNG. First time NEXT GENERATION director Robert Scheerer credited the writing as the source of that episode's success, downplaying his own contribution considerably.

Melinda Snodgrass, a licensed lawyer and a STAR TREK fan of long standing, had already written novels before taking a shot a screenwriting— including the STAR TREK novel THE TEARS OF THE SINGERS. Snodgrass took a shot at television largely at the urging of her friend George RR. Martin, a fine writer in his own right and then involved with CBS' BEAUTY AND THE BEAST television series.

"The Measure of a Man" began its life as a speech script. The day Snodgrass submitted it was the day the Writer's Guild strike went into effect, and Snodgrass threw in the towel and moved back to her native New Mexico. But the script so impressed Maurice Hurley that not only did it wind up on the air, it also led to Melinda Snodgrass becoming a NEXT GENERATION story editor, and then executive story consultant. Starting in December of 1988, Snodgrass was ultimately the person behind such episodes as "The Ensigns of Command," "The High Ground," "Up The Long Ladder," and "Pen Pals."

She also did rewrites for such episodes as "Contagion," which was Doctor Pulaski's big episode, and "Peak Performance," which she saw as a return to the submarine-movie-in-space atmosphere of the classic Trek episode "Balance of Terror." "Peak Performance" also marked director Robert Scheerer's second outing at the helm of THE NEXT GENERATION.

Robert Scheerer, who began his show-business career as a dancer and only later moved on to directing, also credits cast members Patrick Stewart, Jonathan Frakes, and, of course, Brent Spiner. Sheerer got into television early, working with children's programming pioneer Shari Lewis, and has enjoyed a long career which has linked him with such diverse programs as GILLIGAN'S ISLAND, KOLCHAK: THE NIGHT STALKER (the caveman episode), MATLOCK, FALCON CREST, and, ultimately, STAR TREK: THE NEXT GENERATION.

Director Rob Bowman was embarrassed by the monsters in "The Dauphin" as being fairly poor make-up jobs. He also thought that the alien princess' costumes were cheap looking.

"The Royale" was a story that Tracy Torme had devised even before the cast had been signed for THE NEXT GENERATION, but by the time it reached the screen a disgruntled Torme, already packing his bags, had replaced his name with the pseudonym "Keith Mills." Although there are some very amusing character moments in this episode, for many it fell flat.

Torme had intended it as a comedy, but too much of his original idea was lost. The stranded twentieth-century astronaut for whom the imaginary world of "The Royale" was created was, in Torme's original concept, still very much alive when discovered by an Away Team consisting of Riker, Data and Worf; in fact, he was the central character! One can only imagine Torme's dismay at having the protagonist of his script rewritten as a moldering ancient corpse

This drastic switch also obviated the loss of Torme's original conclusion, in which the still-living astronaut decides to stay in his illusive world rather than go back with the Enterprise team. The reasoning behind this alteration was the notion that the role was so good that a guest star would steal the show from the regulars, a compliment of sorts to Torme but, under the circumstances, a rather backhanded one. The notion that the characters were trapped in a hack-written pulp novel was not Torme's idea, either, but he may have found its inclusion a fitting irony.

"Time Squared" was an interesting and intriguing episode, but a lot was left unresolved at its end. Maurice Hurley, practically a martyr to ST-TNG by this point, once again had the rug pulled out from under him; the temporal distortion which produces two Picards moving would have made sense if he had been allowed to use this story as a lead in to "Q Who": Q's interference would have been the cause of all the strangeness, as Q loves messing with Picard's mind. (Everyone needs a hobby.)

Maurice Hurley finally got to proceed with his planned sequel to "The Neutral Zone" with "Q Who." It was left to the viewers to make the connection between the Borg and the strange destruction of outposts referred to in "The Neutral Zone." Hurley, Berman and Roddenberry worked together to create the Borg, a hive race of humanoid cyborgs that functioned collectively, like a swarm of bees.

John Delancie's Q comes across as a much more ominous character here, although the comic touches, as always, remain memorable, especially when he encounters Guinan. In fact, this episode is notable for its tantalizing glimpses into Guinan's history, but more so for introducing an unbeatable foe and leaving both cast and viewers with a feeling for the true depth of space and the many hazards it might contain.

# A LITTLE CONTROVERSY

STAR TREK: THE NEXT GENERATION aroused the ire of the anti-abortion crowd with Melinda Snodgrass's episode "Up The Long Ladder." Here, a race of clones suffering from too much replication steals DNA from Riker and others in order to add genetic diversity and strengthen their race.

Riker, outraged, destroys the clones made form his cells and Crusher's. This struck right-to-life viewers as a pro-choice stance. And while Snodgrass did not intend the clone destruction scene as such, she certainly intended Riker's motivations as such, giving him a speech decrying the fact that he— his body— was used against his will when it was cloned, in direct contravention of his stated desires.

The Bowman-directed "Manhunt" had originally been intended as another film noir holodeck episode by writer Tracy Torme, but matters were altered by a powerful force: Gene Roddenberry's wife, Majel Barrett, who returned as Lwaxana Troi and drew the focus of the episode to herself. (She also requested Bowman specifically as director for the project.)

Tracy Torme wasn't really bothered by the Lwaxana Troi aspect of the script, but was appalled to see his carefully-wrought Dixon Hill portions swept under the carpet. Torme was particularly fond of his Chandleresque narration, intended to be spoken by Patrick Stewart, but this was cut entirely. With what he felt was some of his best writing left in the dust of the cutting room floor, Torme took his name off the episode, which bears the pseudonym "Terry Devereux." He had no desire for anyone to associate the final product as a result of his writing.

## GREY IS BORING

If the first season closer, "The Neutral Zone," was a bit dull and pointless, then there are no words whatsoever sufficient to describe the utter dreariness of the second season finale, "Shades of Grey." Riker gets sick; Pulaski struggles to save him while Deanna emotes fretfully; Riker relives clips from the first two seasons.

It is difficult to understand why an episode this bad was made, other than the obvious savings in shooting time. Why they chose to end the season with it and leave a sour taste in the minds of viewers everywhere is. Rob Bowman had little to say about the episode beyond the fact that he shot it in three days. (He didn't even get to pick the clips; that honor went to Eric Stillwell.)

The second season of ST-TNG was a short one, totaling only twenty-two episodes, which disturbed head honcho Rick Berman, as did the unhappy fact that most of the episodes were rushed; matters would improve in this regard with the next season.

## ABANDON SHIP

By season's end, Tracy Torme, fed up with what he'd been put through regarding his scripts for "Manhunt" and "The Royale," had already left the show. At season's end, so did many writers and producers like John Mason, Scott Rubinstein, Leonard Moldinow, Michael Gray, Burton Armus, and Robert McCullough. Perhaps the most notable departure was that of Maurice Hurley, who threw in the towel and moved on to what he hoped would be greener pastures.

Many, such as Melinda Snodgrass, who remained with ST-TNG through the following season, felt that Hurley's contribution had been the major strength of the second year of the series. However, Hurley seems to be the obvious unnamed person who Tracy Torme saw as his opponent on a number of issues, including the topical references in "Conspiracy."

Torme was certain that the individual, who he does not identify, meddled with Torme's scripts in a spiteful manner, as Torme, thanks to his 'creative consultant' status, could not be fired by that person; but the person, who was leaving at the end of the second season, could stymie Torme's writing. Whether this was Maurice Hurley or not, there were other aspects to Torme's disgruntled feelings. Eventually, Rick Berman asked Torme to return to ST—TNG, an offer Torme would graciously decline.

Hurley's own stated reason for leaving was that he felt that he had met the challenge of working on the show, and considered it time to move on to other labors. Whatever the real reasons behind his departure, and despite some friction with some staff members, Hurley had helped ST-TNG immeasurably during his two year tenure. Fortunately, matters would only continue to improve during the third season without his influence.

# *BEHIND THE SCENES: YEAR THREE*

Replacing Maurice Hurley at the beginning of the third season was Michael Wagner. He contributed ideas to episodes including the season opener "Evolution," but didn't remain with the show for long. In his three weeks with THE NEXT GENERATION, Wagner hired Michael Piller, who soon found himself as the head writer/producer of the series.

Piller, who had worked as a programming executive (aren't those the guys who allegedly killed the original STAR TREK series?), journalist and as a writer on SIMON AND SIMON (with Maurice Hurley), became an important force in the series' continuing development. Hans Beimler and Richard Manning remained with the show, showing a remarkable longevity. They had almost left during the first season, and were almost fired the second, but now they found themselves in the positions of co-producers.

Other third season changes in staff included the debut of Marvin Rush, the new director of photography. A documentary and sitcom cameraman, Rush first achieved prominence as a cameraman on the original WKRP IN CINCINNATI, and would work as director of photography on EASY STREET (a short-lived series with WKRP star Loni Anderson), THE TRACY ULLMAN SHOW, DEAR JOHN, and another WKRP-connected show, Tim Reid's late, lamented FRANK'S PLACE.

After being involved in a couple of go-nowhere films (THE RUNNIN' KIND and MEET THE HOLLOW-HEADS— anybody remember either of these?), he was interviewed by David Livingston and Rick Berman, who were impressed by his work on FRANK'S PLACE. Rush leaped at the chance to work on THE NEXT GENERATION.

## READY. . SET. . GO

The season opener, "Evolution," found the Enterprise crew wearing more comfortable, cotton uniforms. It also brought back Gates McFadden as Dr. Beverly Crusher. No explanation was given for the departure of Pulaski (maybe no one cared) or for why Crusher returned. This might have been because the change in medical personnel was rather abrupt; Michael Piller wrote Crusher back into the script, which, along with a number of others in the works, started out being written with Pulaski as ship's doctor. (With McFadden back on THE NEXT GENERATION, Diana Muldaur was free to head, eventually, for L.A. LAW, where yet another abrupt departure would ultimately claim her.)

In approaching "Who Watches The Watchers," director Robert Wiemer was a bit concerned that the show's message, which somewhat obviously stated the reductionist viewpoint that religion equals ignorant superstition, might offend some viewers, but this never seemed to be the case. Instead, it turned out to be a gripping story where Picard found himself in the awkward position of being considered a god by some Mintakans when they discover a Federation observation near their village, and witness such miracles as Starfleet personnel beaming up and down.

Of course, this was a pet issue of Roddenberry's. "I've always thought," said Roddenberry, "that if we did not have supernatural explanations for all the things [that] we might not understand right away, this is the way we would be, like the people on that planet." Roddenberry further detailed his feelings on this subject:

"I was born into a 'supernatural' world in which all my people— my family— usually said, 'That is because God willed it,' or gave other supernatural explanations for whatever happened. When you confront those statements on their own, they just don't make sense. They are clearly wrong. You need a certain amount of proof to accept anything, and that proof was not forthcoming to support those statements."

Roddenberry was rather disappointed at the lack of response to "Who Watches The Watchers," having hoped, perhaps to generate some degree of controversy over it, if not to outright convert viewers to his ultra rational but grossly oversimplified views on the subject. "It is a source of considerable amusement to me that we can do shows like this and on various other subjects, large and small, and get little or no public reaction. If these things were to be done on Broadway or in motion pictures, they would have stunned audiences. The audiences would have said, 'How wild, how forward, how advanced.' But because these subjects are done on a syndicated television show, in our time slot, no one really notices them.

"I thought several times that the world of drama would have stood up and cheered us," Roddenberry continued in an interview which appeared in THE HUMANIST magazine shortly before his death, "but no, only silence. But there is one advantage, one thing happening: all of these episodes are brought back and rerun every year. What will happen with STAR TREK: THE NEXT GENERATION is almost identical to what happened to the original STAR TREK, as larger and larger audiences become acquainted with the program.

"The original STAR TREK audience now says, 'Hurrah, what fine shows.' This has brought us considerable pleasure that they would notice it. STAR TREK: THE NEXT GENERATION is on that same path now and more so. The time will come when the second series will attain its true stature. I just hope some of it happens while I'm still alive; I'm not jealous that I don't have praise. This happens very broadly in contacts with humans. The world is not necessarily poorer because a painter or playwright is not recognized in his or her lifetime."

A certain sense of self-importance permeates these seemingly humble words of the late Gene Roddenberry, would-be philosopher. Perhaps, in time, successive reruns of "Who Watches the Watchers" and other issue-oriented STAR TREK episodes will cause the world to sit up and take notice of Gene Roddenberry after all, and place him among the pantheon of such great Twentieth-Century thinkers as Freud, Heidegger, Sartre and Einstein.

On the special-effects front of "Who Watches The Watchers," the Federation observation post which plays such a pivotal role in the story was composited by special effects whiz Rob Legato in post production, a seemingly seamless hidden chamber inside a rock outcropping in the Vasquez Rocks; the ceiling of the secret installation, seemingly carved out of the same rocks, was actually constructed out of a rumpled paper grocery sack.

A great job on the Planet Hell set by first time director David Carson highlighted "The Enemy," a Romulan episode, which features a welcome and dramatic aberration from the general niceness of THE NEXT GENERATION regulars when Worf refuses to give a wounded Romulan a transfusion of his own blood.

This idea was put forward by Michael Piller, who received a somewhat stunned response at that particular story conference. This decision was consistent with Klingon nature, which was fortunately given more precedence than any concerns about undermining STAR TREK's veneer of civilization! Other writers thought that Piller was about to destroy the character of Worf.

Even Michael Dorn was taken aback at the idea; he thought, at first, that Worf's honor would drive him to contribute the blood despite his hatred for Romulans. But Dorn eventually came around, realizing that this was a perfect opportunity to remind viewers that Worf was not, after all, human, and to explore this difference in fairly powerful terms. Dorn now counts "The Enemy" as one of his favorite episodes, because even though he only has three scenes, they are among the best he's ever played in terms of revealing new aspects of his Klingon alter ego.

Originally, "The Enemy" was a story in which Geordi LaForge and Deanna Troi were stranded on a hostile planet; Troi's involvement was later dropped, and she remained on board the Enterprise, and the Romulans were reintroduced. This was Michael Piller's idea, as the quest for worthy antagonists for Picard and crew was still underway.

Unsatisfied with the use of the Romulans in "The Neutral Zone" and "Contagion," Piller went back to view their appearances on the classic STAR TREK, and decided to bring them back with the old shows as his inspiration. To strengthen their presence, he decided to have certain Romulan characters recur on a regular basis, a theory put into practice a short time later when the Romulan commander from "The Enemy" again appeared in "The Defector."

Marina Sirtis was a bit annoyed at her exclusion from this episode; in the first script draft she read of this episode, it was her character, Deanna, who got the better of the Romulan while Geordi was blind. The final script left her one line, which never even made it to the final cut, making "The Enemy" a completely Troi-less episode. Sirtis sees this as part of STAR TREK's continual letdown of the entire female portion of the human race.

The director of "The Enemy," David Carson, had worked with Marina Sirtis extensively in British television, including a Sherlock Holmes episode; Carson directed a number of episodes of that series, show in this country on public television's MYSTERY.

In the worst of the Roddenberry tradition, "The High Ground" clumsily addresses topical issues, in this case what has long been referred to by historians as 'The Irish Question.' Even so, its action sequences are among the best of the series. But writer Melinda Snodgrass did not originally want to use the conflict between Great Britain and Northern Ireland as the model for this episode's conflict.

What she had in mind was the American Revolution; the Romulans would have been aiding the rebels as the French did the colonists, and Picard would have been in the position of the British general Cornwallis! An intriguing idea, but too obscure for television viewers, reasoned the producers, who told a reluctant Snodgrass to go with the Irish model.

Jonathan Frakes stepped behind the camera to direct Rene Echeverria's script of "The Offspring," a moving story in which Data creates a daughter for himself. On the other hand, then script consultant Melinda Snodgrass didn't care for it at all, perhaps an excessive reaction, but she was correct in pointing out certain similarities to "The Measure of a Man": Starfleet's attempts to take Lal away from Data seem to indicate that the legal precedent regarding sentient beings set in the earlier episode doesn't carry much weight after all. Jonathan Frakes certainly proved he was a good director with this episode.

An episode made most engaging by the appearance of ex A-TEAM loony Dwight Schultz's portrayal of Barclay, "Hollow Pursuits" examines an interesting subject: holodeck abuse. Writer Sally Caves also provided a first for ST-TNG: we actually see Counselor Troi counseling someone.

A bit of Federation back-history was tossed out in "Sarek," when Picard revealed that he'd been at Spock's wedding; this was also THE NEXT GENERATION's first reference to Spock. It was not to be the last.

"Menage A Troi," in which Riker, Deanna and Lwaxana are kidnapped by a Ferengi in love with the elder Troi, was originally inspired by O. Henry's classic story "The Ransom of Red Chief," in which a pair of kidnappers are eventually tormented by their intended victim. But the script, co-written by Gene Roddenberry's assistant Susan Sackett along with Fred Bronson, soon lost track of this.

Once again Majel Barrett attempted, and sadly succeeded, in pulling the rug out from under THE NEXT GENERATION; Sackett and Bronson actually developed the story with Roddenberry, and his hand lies heavy across it.

Tom Benko was another ST-TNG regular to move up to the directorial chair; in his case, he moved up from his position as a film editor for the show, a job which he has held since "Encounter At Farpoint." Benko had also had some experience as an assistant director (including a stint on, of all shows, BATTLESTAR GALACTICA!), but he was obliged to wait three years before his shot at a STAR TREK: THE NEXT GENERATION episode.

"Transfigurations," wherein a fugitive, evolving alien is saved and befriended by Beverly Crusher, apparently had a love scene between Crusher and the fugitive. The scene was vetoed in yet another case of romanticus interruptus for the good doctor. Benko was bothered, but this cut did not prevent him from doing a good job.

By the time "The Best of Both Worlds" aired as the season finale/cliffhanger, there was considerable speculation that Patrick Stewart might not return for the fourth season of ST-TNG. He had expressed some unhappiness with what little he was given to do with the character of Jean-Luc Picard. Picard's transformation into the Borg Locutus, devised by Michael Piller, certainly left that option open. (An earlier idea, dropped as nonsensical, had the Borg recombining Data and Picard into one entity!) The story certainly seemed more than ready to put Riker in charge, and Jonathan Frakes seemed more than adequate for the task.

Whatever happened behind the scenes here, he did return, and he would have plenty to do during the fourth season. Also considered as a regular character was Shelby, played by Elizabeth Dennehy, but this idea was eventually nixed. It was decided to develop a new series regular from the ground up. If nothing else, "The Best of Both Worlds" showed that THE NEXT GENERATION creative team had finally learned something from the pathetically weak endings of the first two seasons.

## END OF THE SEASON

The end of the third season did see some personnel departures, however, and, as might be expected, they were largely among the writing staff: producer Ira Behar and story editors Richard Manning and Hans Beimler all went their separate ways. Ron Moore moved up to the position of executive script consultant, while Michael Piller retained his place as executive producer in charge of scripts.

One of the composers involved in ST-TNG was Dennis McCarthy, who previously had scored portions of the original V miniseries and all of the series episodes. By the end of the third season, McCarthy had scored thirty-six episodes including the pilot "Encounter at Farpoint," with a grand total of nineteen hours of music under his belt.

Trading off episodes with Dennis McCarthy was Ron Jones, who took his task composing a score for "The Best of Both Worlds, Part One" very seriously. The producers were a bit overwhelmed by his score, however; Jones had striven to create a feeling of impending doom which exceeded any threatening music of all previous STAR TREK episodes old and new. He succeeded, but perhaps too well, as they asked him to tone it down a bit!

The end of the third season also saw the departure of executive story consultant Melinda Snodgrass, who left because of the many restraints put on her as a writer by the show's written-in-stone rules and regulations. Sick of having her hands tied, she returned to New Mexico to concentrate on novel writing. During her tenure on ST-TNG, Snodgrass had written mostly strong character-themed shows, avoiding such devices as the Holodeck, which she felt was a weak dramatic premise. (But then, she never wrote for Barclay.) The loss of Snodgrass was an unfortunate one for the series, but others would carry on.

A little publicized clash between the old guard of STAR TREK and the new NEXT GENERATION occurred during the shooting of the motion picture STAR TREK V: THE FINAL FRONTIER. William Shatner, long prone to denigrate the new series, was now a bit nervous that it might steal the thunder of his new film, his first as a director.

Shatner's insecurities at the helm of STAR TREK V are legendary. When Will Wheaton, who played Wesley Crusher on THE NEXT GENERATION, walked across the Paramount lot to visit the soundstage where Shatner was shooting, he was accorded a less than warm reception. When Shatner discovered that Wheaton was a member of the cast of THE NEXT GENERATION, the older actor mercilessly mocked the notion of a child on the bridge of 'his' ship, the Enterprise. This caused the sixteen-year old Wheaton to leave the movie set in tears. After all, the teenager had been mocked by an actor who had been something of a hero to him.

When Gene Roddenberry heard of this incident of petty cruelty, he was understandably incensed, and furiously contacted Harve Bennett, who was, for the last time, producing a STAR TREK theatrical film. His words to producer Bennett regarding Shatner were reportedly the following: "He's your problem now, not mine." Shatner was to apologize to Will Wheaton soon after insulting him, but there is little to indicate that either of them have forgotten the incident, much less enough to regard the other as a friend.

# BEHIND THE SCENES: YEAR FOUR

By the start of the fourth season, Gene Roddenberry had graciously fallen back and Rick Berman was running the ship. According to many people, Roddenberry was still an integral Piller of the show, but the simple truth of the matter was this: Rick Berman was the guy who was really running things. Berman had, of course, been involved with the show from the beginning, coming to it directly from a position as a vice president in charge of special projects for Paramount Studios.

After working with Robert Justman throughout most of the first season, Rick Berman quickly became a co-executive producer. As Roddenberry moved farther and farther from the center of his own universe, Berman began to exert more control. Fortunately, it was Berman who was responsible for the vast improvements that made the third, and then the fourth, seasons of STAR TREK: THE NEXT GENERATION as excellent as they were.

Berman realized that a good show starts in the writing process, and he made better stories one of his priorities. In addition to working with the writing team, Berman oversees practically every aspect of STAR TREK: THE NEXT GENERATION, before, during and after production.

## NEW WRITERS

Michael Piller, the producer in charge of scripts, hired a number of writers for the fourth season. Most notable, perhaps, was Jeri Taylor, who wrote for such diverse programs as MAGNUM P.I., JAKE AND THE FAT MAN, IN THE HEAT OF THE NIGHT, and QUINCY. Taylor had never seen any STAR TREK episodes, old or new, when she landed this job, and she spent quite a few hours in front of her television brushing up on background for her new job.

With the cost per episode in the general neighborhood of one and a half million dollars, ST-TNG was, still, by this point, making money for Paramount, with daily reruns in almost every city showing the series— and a good market around the world, as well.

Writer Michael Piller started working on "The Best of Both Worlds II" without as much as an inkling of how he was going to defeat the Borg. Composer Ron Jones continued his work in the second half of the Borg-two parter, and plans were even set in motion to release the complete score on compact disc.

## BEST AND WORST

One of the best, and, dramatically speaking, most daring NEXT GENERATION episodes was "Family," the thoughtful coda to "Best of Both Worlds." It was also the lowest rated show of the fourth season. However, writer Ronald Moore and director Les Landau had nothing to be ashamed of. Patrick Stewart shone in this episode which featured veteran British actor Jeremy Kemp as his spiteful older brother and the eternally classy Samantha Eggar as his sister-in-law. "Family" is the only STAR TREK story to date which doesn't even show the bridge of the Enterprise.

Michael Piller had hoped to make "The Best of Both Worlds" a three part story, as he wasn't entirely certain that Picard was really all right at the end of that episode, but that idea was vetoed by his superiors, who claimed that the show was, generally speaking, not a week-to-week serial like L.A. LAW.

Piller, like many viewers of the show, felt that this was not an appropriate place for a quick-fix, everything-is-back-to-normal-at-story's-end approach, and convinced Rick Berman and Gene Roddenberry to do a sequel, of sorts. Even so, Berman insisted on a science fiction subplot going on aboard the Enterprise. Piller eventually had his way, with all the plots involving family relationships. Only the Wesley-meets-his-dad holodeck plotline, from an idea by Suzanne Lambdin and Bryan Stewart, distracted from the principal plot. It was weak but did tie in to the overall theme of the episode.

"Family" was one episode shot largely on location: the Picard family's French estates were actually a house in Encino, California and a vineyard in Palmdale, in the heat of the desert. "Family" also marks the revelation of Transporter Chief O'Brien's first name: Miles. Actor Colm Meaney was relieved, for the show's writers had long threatened to christen the character 'Aloysius.'

A highlight of the fourth season was to be the episode "Brothers," another great Data episode. Veteran actor Key Luke, who appeared in David Carradine's KUNG FU series at one point in his long and illustrious career, was originally considered for the role of Dr. Noonian Soong, but the part ultimately went to Brent Spiner, who really shone in the triple role.

"Brothers" was also the first episode to be scripted by executive producer Rick Berman. But Berman's original story did not have Lore appearing in it, which led Michael Piller, as executive producer in charge of the writing for ST-TNG, to find the Data/Soong confrontation a bit talky and potentially boring. The third character basically forced his way into the show, which is just as well, as this addition (by Michael Piller) lead to an extremely watchable episode.

A bit of controversy was stirred, albeit briefly, with "Suddenly Human." The episode seemed like it was about to delve into the question of child abuse when the Enterprise rescues a human teenager who had been raised by an alien race and completely assimilated into their culture. Old, healed injuries arouse Picard's suspicions, along with the viewer's fear that THE NEXT GENERATION was about to veer into another "topic-of-the-week," only to boil down to just another Prime directive question. Some viewers actually thought that there was evidence of child abuse in the story, originally by Ralph Phillips. Michael Piller defended the show against angry letters, insisting that there had been no abuse and that it was just a case of poor plot comprehension.

Producer Lee Sheldon wasn't with ST-TNG for long, but before he left behind the script for "Remember Me," in which Beverly Crusher finds herself trapped in a Phildickian nightmare. (He also recommended Jeri Taylor to Michael Piller, who hired her as his second in command after she did a rewrite for the script of "Suddenly Human.")

A strange humor permeates Sheldon's sole contribution, especially when Crusher's shrinking universe has dwindled to the Enterprise bridge, where the unflappable alternative Picard adapts immediately to every change while Crusher verges on the edge of panic. Interestingly enough, this story had been considered as a subplot for "Family" but was wisely done as a separate episode.

The underground tunnels in "Legacy," which introduced Tasha Yar's treacherous sister, were actually the sets from the Borg ship, redressed for this episode.

# DIRECTOR FRANKS

Jonathan Frakes directed yet another excellent episode with "Reunion," another Klingon classic which aroused some ire by bumping off Worf's love interest K'Ehleyr. Michael Piller takes full credit or blame for this. Although it was unfortunate to lose Susie Plakson, her character's death does provide the dramatic impetus for Worf's revenge.

The genesis of "Future Imperfect" was a simple proposal by writers David Carren and Larry Carroll. Basically, Michael Piller bought the story on a brief verbal description of nothing more than the story's teaser— and soon afterwards, he gave the two writers jobs on the staff. The shooting of this script proceeded so well that they found that it was actually running short— so instead of having their script cut, these new writers were asked to write an additional scene.

They wrote a scene with Riker and his "son" in an elevator, which became an integral, in fact essential, portion of the story. (Carren had previously written for the Gil Gerard BUCK ROGERS series of the seventies, while Carroll has a special place in cinematic history as the film editor of THE TEXAS CHAINSAW MASSACRE). The underground Romulan hideout in "Future Imperfect" was, once again, the Borg set, still doing duty long after "The Best Of Both Worlds."

"Final Mission" was originally intended to take place on an ice world, but budgetary considerations made a desert location shoot more feasible. In an interesting piece of casting, former SPACE: 1999 actor Nick Tate guests as Captain Drago, but dies off fairly quickly, leaving Wesley, once again, to save the day. Rick Berman cites the fountain effects, done largely on location, as one of the most difficult effects problems of the series. This episode is well remembered as the one where Wesley finally leaves the Enterprise.

In "The Loss," another strange space phenomenon causes Deanna Troi to lose her empathic abilities, which to her is equivalent to losing an entire sense, and becomes, in the words of one person involved in the show, a "super-bitch." Needless to say, by the end of the story everything was hunky-dory again.

Because STAR TREK: THE NEXT GENERATION episodes all too frequently end with such a happy reversion to the status quo, no matter what the crisis, executive producer Michael Piller actually considered depriving Troi of her empathic abilities on a permanent basis. This was too drastic a move, and she got it all back. . . what a surprise!

The basic idea for "Data's Day" had been around ever since Harold Apter proposed a Picard story with a similar structure; eventually, Data became the lead, for the simple reason that he's the only character on the show who is up and running all around the clock. The Romulan spy subplot was introduced at Rick Berman's assistance in order to keep the story from seeming fragmentary.

For director Robert Wiemer, the greatest problem in bringing the story of "Data's Day" to the screen was the producers' insistence on the importance of showing Data's cat. Wiemer was convinced that having an animal in the shoot would be more trouble than it was worth.

However, the cat was apparently very professional, and matters proceeded without a hitch. Perhaps a bit more complex, but ultimately more effective, was the scene where Beverly Crusher teaches Data the rudiments of ballroom dancing in preparation for O'Brien's wedding to Keiko. Gates McFadden, an accomplished dancer, did all the choreography for the scene. Most of the dialogue in the dance-lesson scene was improvised by Brent Spiner and Gates McFadden, while Data's huge grin was put in at the suggestion of Wiemer.

As for O'Brien's wedding, there had been some talk of introducing a new female character to serve as a replacement for Wesley Crusher and as a romantic foil for O'Brien. But rather than develop a new lead, they created the role of Keiko (Rosalind Chao), a ship's botanist, and married her to O'Brien. Part of this was spurred by their desire to have a recurring character (or two) involved in the process of raising a family. Earlier plans to marry off Picard never quite jelled.

## HIGHEST RATED ST-TNG

Another revived script from Paramount's aborted STAR TREK II television series of the late '70s, "Devil's Due"— reworked to give Picard a strong female foil— was the highest rated episode of STAR TREK: THE NEXT GENERATION since "Encounter at Farpoint." Rewritten by Phil Lazebnik, this episode also had uncredited writing input from Michael Piller, David Carren, Melinda Snodgrass and Lee Sheldon.

Strangely close to the original STAR TREK in spirit, this was a fun episode which was not spoiled by too many hands. The antagonist's gender was changed from the original, becoming Ardra, a gorgeous woman who locks horns with Captain Picard. "Devil's Due" was the second ST-TNG story to be directed by series film editor Tom Benko, who enjoys his regular job but finds directing more challenging.

"Clues" is a NEXT GENERATION story with an intriguing origin: the original spec script was submitted by Bruce D. Arthurs a mailman in Phoenix, Arizona. Reworked by Joe Menosky, it provided director Les Landau with a bit of a challenge, since its mystery plot involved repeating the same sequence of events four times in the episode! Menosky's dialogue improvements led to his employment on the show staff. (Arthurs, one presumes, is still delivering mail in Phoenix.)

Although based on a story by Marc Scott Zicree, "First Contact" did not retain much of Zicree's original idea beyond the fact that the warp scientist in the story was a woman (Carolyn Seymour played the part) and that she left her planet at the end of the story. Michael Piller realized that for the story to work, it had to be turned completely around and shown from the point of view, not of the Enterprise crew, but of the alien culture being investigated. Of course it was necessary to get Rick Berman's approval for such a format-breaking ploy. Berman went along with the idea— as long as they never did it again.

Although it was taken out of his hands, Mark Scott Zicree was pleased with the way the episode turned out. At earlier stages in its development, "First Contact" had been a candidate for the third season cliffhanger, and at one point as the episode where Wesley left the Enterprise— as an exchange student to the planet below! An even more intriguing idea would have been, in essence, a parody of STAR TREK fandom, in which the Enterprise crew became famous on the planet below, prompting a wave of Federation-inspired fashions!

On the other hand, Zicree wasn't too crazy about the scene in which an alien woman helps Riker escape only if he'll have sex with her. Michael Piller, who came up with the scene, enlisted CHEERS' Bebe Neuwirth (she spent four hours getting her makeup put on for her short scenes) to bring the scene to life, and most viewers found it an amusingly bizarre incident in the history of Trek.

The episode "Galaxy's Child," in which the Enterprise accidentally kills a whale-like space creature only to have its newborn baby imprint on the ship, was scripted by former NEXT GENERATION producer Maurice Hurley. This story line was boosted by a Leah Brahms subplot (uncredited) by Jeri Taylor from an idea by Thomas Kartozian. Geordi LaForge actually meets the real Leah Brahms, who is nothing like her holodeck alter ego as seen in "Booby Trap," a plot which gives LeVar Burton more than a few good comic moments as his expectations are dashed and he strives to befriend someone who isn't exactly what he wanted her to be. In an unusual move, much of the space creature special effects were done utilizing computer animation, an effect ST-TNG generally avoids.

## SOME FAILED

The generally high quality of the fourth season took a painful plunge downwards with "Night Terrors." Deanna has allegedly terrifying but really lame-looking flying dreams. Michael Piller, somewhat apologetically, is on record as claiming that the show was weak because everyone was still getting their 'space legs' after taking time off for the Christmas season.

Jonathan Frakes, not one to mince words, described Deanna's flying scenes as "shitty," and the episode itself as boring. Resident NEXT GENERATION special effects chief Rob Legato was a bit embarrassed by the effects involved but pointed out that flying never looks right. One can only hope that Marina Sirtis will never again be obliged to hang from wires as she did here

"Identity Crisis," has an alien virus threatening to transform Geordi. It went into serious overtime when it came time to shoot on the "Planet Hell" set: seventeen hour days were called for, and the episode went half a day beyond schedule nevertheless.

## FRAKES SHINES

Easily the best of Jonathan Frakes' consistently good outings as director, "The Drumhead" is probably one of the best ST-TNG episodes of all time. For all its complexity, it was a bottle show, and Frakes brought it in at a quarter of a million dollars under budget, which most certainly endeared him to Paramount! Ron Moore had proposed the basic witch-hunt idea, but the script as finished was entirely Jeri Taylor's.

Considering Jean Simmons' distinguished career, on would think that STAR TREK would be beneath her. . . but in fact, she apparently watches STAR TREK: THE NEXT GENERATION with an almost religious fervor.

"The Host" was filmed while Gates McFadden, whose Beverly Crusher is a central character of the episode, was pregnant. She was shot by strategically placing the camera, or as Jonathan Frakes succinctly put it, by filming her "from her boobs up."

Rush cast the additional characters for the episode, including Franc Luz, who played Odan, or, rather, the first body occupied by Odan. The character also had to be played by Jonathan Frakes, so Rush, Frakes and guest star Luz worked together to develop the character. This was Jonathan Frakes' first portrayal of a different character on the series. (Although it does seem that everyone eventually gets to play someone else; Brent Spiner still has quite a lead on everybody else in this regard, however!) Since the character was described in detail in the script, the actors had a concrete idea to work from.

Rush was further overwhelmed that the show's producers would assign him such a heavily dramatic story his first time out. He somewhat downplays the quality of his effort on this outing, although he did a very good job; it was the script which faltered, in the end. Rush rather obliquely acknowledged this, but did not see it as his place to tamper with the story.

The episode "The Mind's Eye" featured Geordi LaForge's kidnapping and brainwashing by Romulans planning to assassinate a Klingon leader (with a little help from treacherous Klingons). Line producer David Livingston stepped in as director for this episode, his first in that position. This was the script he hoped he'd get his first time out.

Some have compared "The Mind's Eye" to the John Frankenheimer classic The Manchurian Candidate, a similarity that Livingston himself was not unaware of; he actually desired to find someone from the cast of that film and use them in the episode but settled for introducing a *hommage* shot in the scene where a brainwashed Geordi kills a holodeck version of O'Brien. The episode featured various bizarre visual effects, as seen through the distorted viewpoint of the Romulan-controlled Geordi's visor.

Matters were aided considerably by LeVar Burton's efforts in this episode, playing his regular character but with a considerable spin in the portrayal, particularly in the brainwashing sequence, a really grueling bit of work culminating in a bloodcurdling scream. The writers of the episode had gone against the scream, but Livingston prevailed, and was quite pleased with the final result of his first directorial effort.

Following Jonathan Frakes' lead, Patrick Stewart made his directorial debut with "In Theory," the long-planned Data love story. Stewart didn't quite get off to the great start Frakes did. The story is a bit plodding in its development and is further hindered by an Enterprise-in-danger subplot.

## SEASON FINALE

"Redemption" marked ST-TNG's liberation from stock movie footage of Klingon vessels, as a new top-of-the-line Klingon cruiser was unveiled in this season's unresolved finale. Not a cliffhanger in the strict sense (as "The Best of Both Worlds" was), it reintroduced Denise Crosby to the series, but with no clue as to her identity. It also featured a remarkable number of sets and visuals. Fortunately, money had been saved by doing less expensive episodes such as "The Drumhead," making the Klingon Great Hall a possibility along with various Klingon residences, along with the new Klingon cruiser.

# BEHIND THE SCENES: YEAR FIVE

The fifth year of THE NEXT GENERATION opened with some considerable excitement! There was a rumored appearance by Leonard Nimoy— as Spock— in the works. It was also marred by the death of Gene Roddenberry, some time shortly before the two parts of "Unification" were aired in November. The crossover episode bore a dedication to Roddenberry, and the show would continue to bear a posthumous Gene Roddenberry "executive producer" credit on every episode in honor of the man who created the show.

Berman noted Roddenberry's passing with these words: "What [Roddenberry] created in his lifetime is certainly going to continue. His death is not going to in any way stop the flow of his vision. The thrust of our series has always been to continue Gene Roddenberry's vision. It will be easy to keep doing that because we've never stopped doing it."

Jonathan Frakes honored Roddenberry with a full page ad in a Hollywood trade paper which read, in part: "I'm proud to be a part of the family. We all miss our leader, Gene Roddenberry."

The series continued without Roddenberry, although it is interesting to note that the quality of the fifth season was rather inconsistent. Perhaps the strain of creating a special show around Leonard Nimoy disrupted the usual flow of the year's work. Certainly, Paramount's decision to show only reruns of THE NEXT GENERATION during the first months of STAR TREK VI: THE UNDISCOVERED COUNTRY's theatrical release might have bothered the creators of the television series, as it certainly vexed a good many viewers who saw the ploy as blackmail of sorts: "Ya want your STAR TREK, ya gotta go back to the theater and spend six more bucks."

## MUSIC MAN

The fifth season of ST-TNG also brought with it a new sound: the incidental music of composer Jay Chattaway, who replaced Ron Jones as the series' regular writer of music. Chattaway had actually scored four earlier episodes, the first one being "Tin Man," but the fifth season marked his debut as the primary tunesmith of the twenty-fourth century.

Interestingly enough, it was Chattaway who arranged the STAR TREK theme for Maynard Ferguson's big-band jazz album "Conquistador" (not to be confused with the Cecil Taylor Blue Note album of the same name), back in the late nineteen-seventies. In addition to jazz arrangements, Chattaway's background includes scores for mostly low-budget films, including such Chuck Norris vehicles as MISSING IN ACTION, BRADDOCK: MISSING IN ACTION III, and INVASION U.S.A. In a more enlightened vein, he has also scored Jacques Cousteau documentaries for five years, a job he continues at present.

His experience with the Jacques Cousteau documentaries had left him with a considerable collection of aquatic sounds, which he drew upon liberally for scenes involving the whale-like alien creature. For the creature's ambient sound, Chattaway used the digitally sampled sound of the diggeridoo, an aboriginal Australian instrument; there aren't too many diggeridoo players in Los Angeles.

Chattaway quickly learned one key rule: since Starfleet is not a military organization (yeah, right), all musical phrases and sounds associated with the military, such as snare drums (which Chattaway got away with using in the battle sequences of "Tin Man"!) have been tabooed by the show's producers!

Chattaway then scored three fourth-season episodes of ST-TNG: "Remember Me," "The Host," and "In Theory." Chattaway regrets that time considerations prevented him from inserting a musical joke into the score of "The Host": he wanted to toss off a sly rendition of the old song "I've Got You Under My Skin," a fitting touch for that particular tale of parasitic romance.

## THE SCRIPTS

Berman and Piller's story "Ensign Ro" introduced Michelle Forbes as Ensign Ro Laren, a troubled character who's initial abrasiveness would be toned down to a wry sarcasm in subsequent appearances.

"Silicon Avatar" saw the return of the Crystalline Entity, with spanking new visual effects from Rob Legato's crack team. Series composer Jay Chattaway was obliged to watch "Datalore" for inspiration in creating a musical mood for the Crystalline Entity, as the special effects were not ready for "Silicon Avatar" when he was scoring that particular episode.

With "Disaster" it became painfully apparent that THE NEXT GENERATION's fifth season might not be as good as the two preceding it; a space disaster disables the Enterprise, with such cliched results as: Picard is trapped in a turbolift with a group of children! Keiko goes into labor and Worf must help with the delivery! On the positive side, it was well played, with good comic moments, and it at least managed to keep the childbirth and elevator plots separate.

Only two years before "Unification," ST-TNG story editor, Ron Moore, stated absolutely that, after DeForest Kelley and Mark Lenard, there would be no further ST-TNG appearances. Time was to prove this statement wrong. But contrary to popular belief, Leonard Nimoy's return to television Trek was not a spur-of-the-moment thing. When Nick Mancuso of Paramount gathered the creative team for STAR TREK VI: THE UNDISCOVERED about him, he was already planning a ST-TNG episode to serve as a thematic tie-in; a prelude, and, in fact, an advertisement, for the feature film.

Mancuso was planning to go ahead with the idea with or without anyone from the cast of the movie, but Spock, needless to say, was by virtue of his Vulcan longevity, the obvious choice for such a role. By the time the movie was in the proverbial can, Nimoy had decided to take part, if he could, in this scheme. He approached the ST-TNG production team, and promised to participate if the script was good.

Apparently, the story worked up was good enough for Nimoy's critical eye, and he returned to the almost-forgotten world of series television, a hectic workaday schedule that took him back to the feeling of working on the original STAR TREK: a fast-paced, grueling six-day-week of shooting. Nevertheless, he found working with Patrick Stewart, Brent Spiner and the rest of the ST-TNG crew to be a pleasure. Although he was not personally in the scene, he found Mark Lenard's death scene of Sarek to be quite moving. His favorite scene was his final, emotional interaction with Patrick Stewart.

In "The Game," Riker's amorous inclinations bring him under the sway of an alien seductress with a plan, and when his vacation ends he brings a seemingly harmless game on board the Enterprise which actually saps the will of anyone who plays it. Soon everyone is addicted, including Picard, and only a visiting Wesley Crusher can save the day, as Data has been shut down.

With this episode, composer Jay Chattaway was again caught short by the lag between scoring an episode and the post-production special effects. When the visuals for the addictive Game came through, he was bemused to discover that the shapes that gobbled up the discs in the Game looked like tubas! Fortunately, there was adequate time to work up some new musical passages to play with the inspiration provided by the whimsical images of the deadly game.

Director Robert Scheerer recalls "The New Ground" as one of his favorite recent episodes. He cites the work of FAMILY TIES' Brian Bonsall (as Alexander), along with Michael Dorn, as pivotal in making this relationship-oriented episode a success. This marked a trend first hinted at in "Disaster," as the fifth season seemed determined to be The Year of The Child.

Indeed, the kids-in-space theme of season five kicked into high gear with the Joe Menosky-scripted "Hero Worship," in which a traumatized boy (Joshua Harris) attempts to subdue his troubled emotions by emulating Data's android behavior.

Was there a subliminal political message in "Violations," or is the fact that the villain bears an uncanny resemblance to 1992 presidential candidate Jerry Brown merely a coincidence? Will Bill Clinton take the Democratic nomination of the strength of the number of Democratic NEXT GENERATION fans who found themselves unconsciously linking Brown with the image of a 24th-Century brain-rapist? Or is this undue speculation?

At any rate, "Violations" was an intriguing episode to which director Robert Wiemer brought some unusual directorial touches. Although the identity of the villain was obvious despite a lame attempt to toss a red herring in the direction of his father, "Violations" was perhaps most interesting in that it offered some tantalizing glimpses into the personal past lives of some of the Enterprise crew.

With Rick Berman's sanction, Robert Wiemer went well outside the show's usual visual format to create images of a romantic interlude between Deanna Troi and Riker, and of a young Beverly Crusher being taken to view her husband's body by a young (with hair) Jean-Luc Picard. Both sequences have a disjointed, disturbing quality which presages the intrusion of the psychic invader into these dream-like passages.

Eschewing the use of a total post-production, special-effects approach to these scenes, Wiemer attempted to do most of the work up front, as he shot the scenes. Most impressive was the Crusher/Picard sequence, which used wide-angle lenses and unusual camera movements to create a disjointed and apprehensive atmosphere.

Movements in close-up might seem particularly odd because Wiemer actually had the two actors sit on a dolly; rather than walking, they were moved along by the dolly and filmed from the chest up. This created a disturbing sense of "wrong" body movement reminiscent of some of the techniques used by Jean Cocteau in the underworld sequences of his classic black-and-white film Orpheus.

David Livingston returned as director with "Power Play." In common with Livingston's earlier episode, "The Mind's Eye," "Power Play" involved regular characters who were forced by outside forces to become different characters entirely. In this case, the characters in question were Deanna Troi, O'Brien and Data.

This posed a special concern in the case of Data; Brent Spiner had already played a different take on Data, his 'evil twin' Lore, in two episodes (not to mention Noonian Soong). It was therefore important that the possessed Data, while evil and cruel, not share any of the characteristics of the equally unpleasant Lore.

As for Colm Meany, he had to work up a character totally different from the agreeable but sometimes defensively edgy Chief O'Brien, particularly in regard to his character's wife (Rosalind Chao) and child (unnamed stunt baby). In fact, the scenes where the invaders hold the occupants of Ten Forward hostage draws most of its tension from the interaction between the possessed O'Brien (nicknamed Slash by the director and actors) and his confused and fearful wife.

For Deanna-under-control (a.k.a. 'Slugger; Data's evil occupier was referred to as 'Buzz'), Livingston had some interesting, if basic advice for Marina Sirtis: the entity possessing her was a man. When questioned on this, Livingston insisted; after all, he was the director. The result was a hard-edged, masculine, downright vicious character, quite unlike the generously supportive Deanna Troi.

## A SAND-FULL TO HANDLE

This episode also involved considerable shooting on the infamous "Planet Hell" set. The wind effects created serious problems, particularly with the possibility of sand getting into Brent Spiner's requisite yellow contact lenses; Marina Sirtis' makeup was frequently undone by the flying sand and had to be constantly re-applied.

"Power Play" also featured a memorable out-of-control shuttle sequence shot from inside the shuttle. The complete circle executed by the camera inside the tumbling crashed shuttle was inspired, if not borrowed outright, by a scene in the out-of-control boat during the climactic scenes of Martin Scorcese's CAPE FEAR. It was necessary to rent a special piece of equipment to execute this in-production effect, and Livingston and crew were very pleased with the final result.

As for any perceived similarities between "Power Play" and the STAR TREK episode "Return To Tomorrow," well. . . David Livingston maintains that he's never seen it. He was soon back to his regular job anyway. . . keeping uppity NEXT GENERATION producers in line!

In "Ethics," scripted by Ronald D. Moore from a story by Sara and Stuart Charno, Worf's spine is damaged and he considers enlisting his son's aid in committing the Klingon equivalent of hara-kiri. An arrogant doctor comes into conflict with Beverly Crusher over a new technique that has never been tested on humanoids before; eventually, a new spine is grown for Worf and the operation, after a few tense moments, is a success. Gates McFadden, however, was unhappy with the use of her character in this particular narrative, as Dr. Crusher comes off as strident and preachy, as if she had never tried new, untested techniques herself.

With "Outcast," scripted by Jeri Taylor, THE NEXT GENERATION finally tackled a gay theme— NOT!!! Although this story is a well intentioned plea for understanding and tolerance of people with different sexual habits, it was weakened by its remarkable insistence on avoiding anything remotely resembling any situation here on Earth.

The episode strived to work on too levels. To the discerning eye the Gay parallel was clear. Interestingly, shortly before Roddenberry's death, an article appeared in the Gay newspaper THE ADVOCATE in which an assistant on THE NEXT GENERATION stated that a Gay character would be added to the series in its fifth season, and that Gene Roddenberry fully supported this move. For whatever reason, this never came to pass.

"The First Duty" brought Wesley back, or, rather, Picard visits Starfleet Academy, where Wesley has messed up seriously. An interesting episode, and one which shows us Picard's Academy mentor, the crusty old gardener Boothby— portrayed, in an intriguing science-fiction television crossover, by My Favorite Martian star Ray Walston!

In "Imaginary Friend" this season's focus on children rears its ugly head again with yet another kid story, this one involving an alien entity which brings a little girl's imaginary friend into actual existence—but which perceives the adults on board the Enterprise, especially Picard, as the girl's enemy. It wreaks a bit of havoc before Picard explains things and order is restored.

Even the Borg get exposed to the recurring youth angle in "I, Borg," when a damaged adolescent Borg is rescued and learns something about humanity and individuality, another annoying 'underneath, we're all the same episode.

The fifth season reached its dubious conclusion with "Time's Arrow," which appeared, from the trailers, to flirt with being the "Data's Brain" of THE NEXT GENERATION. Data's head, centuries old and quite dead, is discovered in a mysterious cavern excavated under San Francisco, and the Enterprise investigates the mystery. The strength of this one will depend largely on how it is wrapped up when the sixth season begins; it certainly ended with a cornucopia of eerie effects, as Picard and his team follow Data, where they do not know, but undoubtedly to Nineteenth Century San Francisco, where Data has met a slightly younger Guinan and the obligatory Mark Twain. The show missed the boat in this obvious choice, as San Francisco's benevolent madman of the period, the Emperor Norton, would have made an extremely interesting character.

As for what lies ahead in this story, and for THE NEXT GENERATION in general— only time will tell. Both a sixth and a seventh season are promised, but beyond that Paramount may well settle for STAR TREK—DEEP SPACE NINE, assuming that series catches on as well as expected.

# GENERAL ORDER #1
## An Analysis of The Prime Directive

> *A strong common thread linking the original STAR TREK and THE NEXT GENERATION is The Prime Directive. Does this general order really have the best interests of alien races at heart in all instances? Or does it set the Federation not just apart from new alien cultures, but above them?*

**by Wendy Rathbone**

# NON-INTERFERENCE

Y ou are watching a colony of red ants who have built their home in the brick patio outside your back door. They run about their daily lives with a seeming sense of purpose that is almost enviable. They have a social order, a sense of right and wrong, and a keen desire to live. They even appear intelligent. Suddenly one falls into the large, swimming pool in the center of your yard. He struggles but there appears to be no hope. He will drown. Unless you get the net and rescue him.

Being a compassionate human being with a love for life, you save him. Where's the harm in interfering? Then another one runs up your leg. You brush him off, but he does it again and again. "Borg!" you say as you finally squish the sucker. He's only one of thousands. He won't be missed. Where's the harm in interfering? After all, it was self-defense.

Non-interference.is about the highly controversial Prime Directive as it was introduced in STAR TREK and as it continues through the series of STAR TREK—THE NEXT GENERATION.

The good old STAR TREK CONCORDANCE, the fan's bible/dictionary/reference manual by Bjo Trimble, defines the Prime Directive, or General Order Number One. During the early series it was described as: "a wise but often troublesome rule which prohibits Federation interference with the normal development of alien life and societies. It can be disregarded when absolutely vital to the interests of the entire Federation, but the commander who does violate it had better be ready to present a sound defense of his actions."

This definition is murky at best. Left open to interpretation, it would appear that starship captains can pretty much do as they please if they can come up with that "sound defense" and a good lawyer to present it.

On first read-through, I hesitate at the disturbing yet comforting words: "(the Prime Directive) can be disregarded when absolutely vital to the interests of the entire Federation." This ensures that I, a Federation citizen, can rest easy knowing that I am protected by law against, say, alien invasion. If an innocent, baby-lifeform named Vejur comes along destroying everything in its path and threatens Earth, then it's okay to interfere and destroy the irritating child.

However, it also means that in the "interests of the Federation" the alien society's interests are, right away, never considered to be of equal importance or value. This automatically puts the Federation in the role of 'superior'. It would be the height of conceit to publicly apply for superiority over unknown, alien races when the very nature of the Prime Directive asserts that superiority does exist.

On second read-through, I begin to wonder about events which do not directly affect me. What about the safety of the alien society? What if they are destroying themselves without harm to the Federation? What if what they're doing affects no one but the inhabitants of said society? Is it best and safest to keep them in ignorance, allow them to develop nuclear power and pollute their entire world? Allow them to destroy an entire race even if it is their own? These questions are what lead to the controversy.

This controversy is not about General Order Number One keeping alien societies safe from the 'missionary' type of contamination that has occurred on our own world. Or to keep innocent people safe from contamination of alien disease introduced by anthropologists into a society that has no immunities (or medicines) capable of fighting it. Since this has happened to various Aborigine tribes throughout the countries of Earth, (many of these tribes becoming extinct as a result,) the Prime Directive would seem to be in order in those cases. But what does the Prime Directive have to say about rescuing a race from its own stupidity? Or keeping them in the dark for their own good? Therein lies the controversy.

## PRIME DIRECTIVE DILEMMA

It is not illegal to be stupid, but would you just sit around watching while a planet blew itself to kingdom come? Would you if you could do something about it? Would you if the people down there were your relatives or your friends?

The perfect episode to illustrate this dilemma is "Pen Pals." This second season story written by Melinda M. Snodgrass and Hannah Louise Shearer serves up the difficult scenario where the Prime Directive, if interpreted without qualification, would probably ensure the extinction of an alien society. The Enterprise, exploring an area of space where planets "live fast and die hard," unwittingly (through Data) makes contact with an alien girl.

Data's special 'listening' project allows him to hear her message "is anybody out there?" Without asking permission from Picard, Data answers the call and learns over an eight week period that her world is being destroyed by seismic activity. He learns also that her society has no knowledge of interstellar life. Because of this fact, he is breaking the Prime Directive by answering her call even though he has told her nothing about himself.

When Captain Picard is made aware of the situation, he orders Data to cease all communication with the girl. He calls a meeting of department heads to discuss the violation and try to come up with a solution for both the problem of 'interference' and the fact that the girl's world is dying.

## WHAT DO THE CHARACTERS THINK?

Worf believes the Prime Directive is an absolute. Dr. Pulaski disagrees. She says it is too rigid, callous and cold. Captain Picard advises caution because "what we do today may profoundly affect the future. If we could see every possible outcome. . ." Riker: (finishing his sentence) ". . .we'd be gods—which we are not. If there is a cosmic plan, is it not the height of hubris to think we can or should interfere?" (This statement reminds me of an infuriating religious sect where medical aid is not allowed because only God can be allowed to heal a person, and God will heal only if that person was meant to live.) Geordi: "Are they then fated to die?" Troi: "The cosmic plan may allow for us being here."

At this point, Data, who is a machine and not driven by frail human emotions, points out that, "the Draymans are not a subject for philosophy; they are a people." (Interesting that it would take a machine to point this out.) Picard states that the Prime Directive is also there "to protect us—from allowing our emotions to overwhelm us."

The question is raised: Can someone ask for help from someone they don't know? Apparently, it is not a violation of the Prime Directive to ask for help, but you have to know *who* you're asking.

The discussion goes nowhere, and Picard again orders Data to cease all contact. Data moves to obey. At this point, his hand slips against the volume control (I think it was on purpose) and all in the room suddenly hear the plea for help from what sounds to be a very young and frightened child. The pain of her plea enters their lives.

Suddenly, the situation changes. This is no longer a discussion of philosophical opinion, of cosmic plans. This is personal. No human in his/her right mind can ignore the cries of a helpless individual, especially when that individual is a child begging to be saved. It takes only seconds for the officers to be visibly affected. And in one of the most poignant scenes in all of Trek, Picard goes against all rules he has supposedly upheld and not only gives Data permission for further contact, he also gives him leave to beam down to the transmitter coordinates!

The plot thickens when Data beams back with the girl. Picard is outraged, but nothing can be done. Eventually, after a scientific solution is found to stop the seismic activity on her world, Picard orders Pulaski to wipe the girl's memories. Pulaski's line: "She has to be the person she was born to be" is a little infuriating after her earlier statement inciting the PD to be cold and callous. Who's to say the girl wasn't meant to be the first of her people to contact interstellar life and aid in saving her world? This is, after all, what happened.

The episode raises a few more questions. Why would Data continually disobey the Prime Directive and Picard? Though Data has no emotions, it cannot be said he is without compassion. Still, he had to know he was violating that direct mandate. This is a very serious charge for the android to face. Another question is that of altering a person's memories against their will. Is this moral? This is a very serious god-like act to perform, and rather frustrating when the Prime Directive is supposed to keep the Federation from 'playing god'. The episode does conclude with this thought from Picard: Where the Prime Directive is concerned, we are only human, therefore imperfect.

Another episode where the Prime Directive is mentioned in an interesting way is "The Hunted," by Robin Bernheim. In this story, the planet Angosia knows about the Federation and its starships but hasn't joined the Federation. It becomes known to the members of the crew of the Enterprise that the peaceful, passive people of Angosia genetically programmed certain people of their society to become 'soldiers' during a long and violent war.

When the war ended, the soldiers were no longer needed and were sent to a lunar colony to keep society safe from them (since they are programmed killers and Angosian nature is extremely peaceful.) This colony is a glorified prison full of heroes. One escapes because he wishes to be 'free'. He is not a violent man and yet is programmed to be violent, to be the perfect soldier. He uses every bit of knowledge and wisdom he has as a 'perfect soldier' to elude the Enterprise and the law and to fight for his rights against the people who imprisoned him.

After the Enterprise captures and then loses him, (but not until learning his side of the story,) Picard beams down to the planet where this soldier and others he has freed are at a face-off with the citizens of Angosia. The soldiers, with guns aimed, demand their freedom and equal rights. The head of the planet demands that Picard fight the soldiers and help put them back on the lunar colony. In the midst of the face-off, Picard says, "We cannot interfere in the natural course of development of your culture." And, leaving the startled citizens at gun point, he and the Away Team beam up.

Later he makes the point that the Federation will aid them with solving the problem of reversing the genetic programming. Again. . . Picard appears to use the excuse of the Prime Directive simply to edge out of a sticky situation.

According to the definition, he could have aided the citizens by helping them recapture the soldiers. The Angosians, because they are aware of interstellar life, knew who they were asking for help. The fact that they were not yet a part of the Federation made it difficult for the Enterprise crew to deal with them concerning issues of law.

In this case, the Prime Directive protected no one but the Enterprise crew. By enforcing the PD, they didn't have to take sides. It was quite coincidental that Picard only enforced the PD when it was apparent the soldiers had the upper hand. So again, human emotion seems to have been a motivating factor for enforcing or not enforcing the Federation's highest law.

The definition of the PD in the CONCORDANCE includes this: "When a culture has already been tampered with, the Prime Directive permits judicious action to restore balance." This definition comes, of course, from the original STAR TREK series. It is probably there in defense of Captain Kirk, whose reputation for breaking the Prime Directive on many occasions was rather infamous. Of course, it was always justified. . .

## PICARD BREAKS THE PRIME DIRECTIVE

It is interesting to note, that in the episode "The Drumhead," Picard is accused of violating the Prime Directive nine times. Picard is not the type of man who rushes blindly into another world's affairs, nor does he see himself as superior. This is a man who has great respect for all life forms and all cultures, even enemies. We saw an extreme case of this in his reaction to the 'crystal entity' even after it destroyed entire societies.

However, in a complete turn around from his usual demeanor, in the fifth season episode "I, Borg" he is ready to leave an injured Borg to die. When the Borg is rescued, he then plots to program it to destroy the rest of its kind. Since an unofficial state of war exists between the Borg and the Federation, this obvious PD violation might be allowed.

Remember: "It can be disregarded when absolutely vital to the interests of the entire Federation." But again, it is open for debate. There is no obvious right and wrong here, only emotional judgment. To add to our confusion (in a wonderful mimicry of true life), the episode strangely gave us sympathetic insight into the mind of one Borg. Who can say they didn't like Hugh? Now what do we do?

## THE CONTROVERSY CONTINUES

Another excellent episode involving Prime Directive politics is "First Contact" by Dennis Russell Bailey, David Bischoff, Joe Menosky, Ronald D. Moore, Michael Piller and Marc Scott Zicree. This fourth season episode explores the danger and delight of being the first 'aliens from space' to contact a society on the brink of space exploration. Where the PD is concerned, nothing is ever straight-forward. With this episode, the controversy continues.

Riker, who is disguised as one of the indigenous peoples, is injured and taken to a hospital where his true 'alien' form is discovered. This is not how first contact is supposed to happen. Riker's accident caused the contact to be implemented prematurely.

The people who find out about him are fascinated, paranoid, and fearful. Eventually, the planetary government, consisting of a chancellor, supposedly acting in the best interests of his people, feels they are not ready for this big a change in their culture and asks Picard and the Enterprise to leave. Now, not only are Picard and his people playing god, so to speak, but the chancellor is as well. The people never get to vote on it!

Some interesting dialog from this episode deals directly with the Prime Directive.

*Picard* (who has appeared out of thin air in an astrophysicist's lab): "When a society reaches your level of technology, and is clearly about to initiate warp drive, we feel the time is right for first contact. We prefer meeting like this, rather than a random contact in deep space."

*Troi* (who has accompanied Picard): "We've come to you first because you're a leader in the scientific community. Scientists generally accept our arrival more easily than others."

*Picard*: "We almost always encounter shock and fear on this sort of mission. We hope that you will help us to facilitate our introduction."

Then Picard, Troi and the scientist beam up so they can prove to her that they are not a hoax.

Another conversation involving the Prime Directive:

*Picard*: "Chancellor, we are here only to help guide you into a new era. I can assure you, we will not interfere in the natural development of your planet. That is, in fact, our Prime Directive."

*Chancellor*: "I can infer from that 'directive' that you do not intend to share all this exceptional technology with us."

*Picard*: "That is not the whole meaning, but it is part of it."

*Chancellor*: "Is this your way of maintaining superiority?"

*Picard*: "Chancellor, to instantly transform a society with technology would be harmful, and it would be destructive."

*Chancellor*: "You're right, of course."

Later, Picard admits that: "there is no starship mission more dangerous than 'first contact'." Surveillance of a first contact planet is a controversial decision. Another character points out: "However you describe your intentions, you still represent an end to my way of life."

All these points make the issue of the Prime Directive even more overwhelming for individuals to deal with. Irritating as the controversy is, it is even more irritating to me, as a viewer, to watch as one person in a position of power manipulatively keeps those under his influence in ignorance.

The chancellor decides his people aren't ready for first contact. He says he will deliberately delay their warp program. "We will divert more resources to social development and educational programs to prepare for the day when we are ready for first contact." And yet, one of his people *is* ready for first contact. She, the astrophysicist, ends up leaving her world to go with the Enterprise into space.

Aside from the fact that the Enterprise has just aided and abetted a worldwide government conspiracy (a point which incites an uncanny urge to rip up my voter registration card) the episode is well-written, thought-provoking, exceedingly philosophical and wildly, terrifyingly frustrating!

I figure it this way. If I were one of those aliens on some distant planet, and I didn't have advanced technology, and other people were sneaking around watching me struggle and dream one day of the stars being accessible to my great grandchildren, I'd be pissed if I found out I could've had it all myself. All that wonder, all those delicious worlds and new dreams and peace and hope.

I would like to be given a choice, and know options. I would like to know the mystery behind crop circles and UFOs. I would like to be 'counted' as more than just part of a crowd performing some kind of function as yet unknown to itself. Like the ant, if I'm drowning in a pool, I don't want to be watched by Someone Advanced who cannot make a move to help.

# MORE GOVERNMENT INTERFERENCE

It is interesting to note that even in the episode "The Masterpiece Society," (fifth season) written by Adam Belanoff, Michael Piller and James Kahn, there is another government attempting to impose its values on citizens who have been at last exposed to 'beyond'.

This is a group of humans from Earth who set up an artificial colony 200 years ago in order to genetically engineer the "perfect society." Every life form is a part of the master design. The people grow up knowing exactly what they will do as adults.

Now the society is threatened by a stellar core fragment headed their way which will cause their planet to have such violent earthquakes that their artificial colony will be destroyed. The Enterprise contacts them and communicates the problem.

With the Enterprise visit, their perfect society has been 'contaminated' and will never be the same. A physicist who works with Geordi on a solution to divert the core fragment decides she doesn't want to go back to the colony. Others wish to leave as well as soon as they are aware of the Enterprise, the Federation, and everything that is 'out there'.

The colony is so dependent on every other person in it that it will suffer, if not die, because of this 'migration'. The leader does not want his people to leave, but can't force them to stay. The physicist, Dr. Hannah Bates, has some very emotionally charged dialog to deliver. In one line, she refers to the colony's citizens as the victims of "a 200 year old joke." Who can blame her? They've been sheltered from the realities of galactic expansion for generations. Is this 'natural' development?

*Picard*: "Our presence here has had an unintended influence on your society."

*Hannah*: "Who would choose to live in a ship in a bottle?" She asks for the privilege of living to explore as the Enterprise crew does. They cannot deny her.

*Picard*: "If ever we need reminding of the importance of the Prime Directive, it is now."

*Riker*: "The Prime Directive doesn't apply. They're human." (I had never heard this interpretation before. I assume he means they are from Earth, therefore automatically members of the Federation. But. . .???)

*Picard*: "Doesn't it? Our very presence may have damaged, even destroyed their way of life. Now, whether or not we agree with that way of life, whether they're human or not, is irrelevant. We are responsible."

*Riker*: "We had to respond to the threat of the core fragment, didn't we?"

*Picard*: "Of course we did. But in the end, we may have proved just as dangerous to that colony as any core fragment ever could have been."

I disagree with Picard. Is keeping a society and culture intact, even till death, worth the loss of all individual life? Hannah Bates would disagree. She valued her life as an individual. She would not have wanted to sacrifice herself for an outdated concept of a 'perfect society' just because some ancestor of hers decided that would be best for her.

At least with the Enterprise's help, the core fragment was diverted, and lives were saved. These people of this culture retain all their memories, their art, their philosophy, their way of life and can enter into new societies bringing that knowledge with them. Even if the physical colony dissipates, they will survive. I hope even Picard would agree that is preferable to death.

Other episodes which deal with the PD are: "Justice" (first season), "Too Short A Season" (first season), "Symbiosis" (first season), "Who Watches The Watchers" (third season), "The Devil's Due" (fourth season) and "Half A Life" (fourth season.) I'm sure there are more, as the topic is one that never tires of being addressed.

In the end, whether or not I agree with the Prime Directive is still in question. Most people I have talked with agree with it. One friend says, "I have to say for the most part that I agree with the Prime Directive. Without it, what happened (and is still happening) to many of the indigenous peoples of the Earth would be happening in space. What the Klingons in STAR TREK VI—THE UNDISCOVERED COUNTRY accuse the humans of—imposing their 'white' culture on everyone in the galaxy—would run rampant. . . "

However, there is that wonderful Vulcan concept called IDIC (Infinite Diversity in Infinite Combinations.) Without the Prime Directive, everyone would be the same, absorbed much like the Borg race, into one giant, massive culture with all people straining to be alike. And that would be about as bad as Klingons quoting Shakespeare. . . oops, maybe I'll have to rethink that opinion.

References:

1) THE VOYAGE CONTINUES. . . TREK, THE NEXT GENERATION,

  by James Van Hise

2) STAR TREK CONCORDANCE, by Bjo Trimble

3) Much thanks to Amanda M. G. Peacock for her input, and the red ant colony in my backyard.

# MALAISE IN WONDERLAND
## Angst In The Next Generation

*What is it that makes THE NEXT GENERATION click, and what are the internal problems that the series manages to overcome time after time? While some of these problems have existed since the inception of the series, the writers have managed to get around them and sometimes rise above them .*

**by David Gardner**

# MIDLIFE CRISIS

Gene Roddenberry's follow-up to STAR TREK has beaten the odds. In a period when abysmal sequels to films and television shows were cranked out at a phenomenal rate, THE NEXT GENERATION has managed to please not only mainstream audiences but also fans of the original series. It consistently places high in the ratings and is as popular among fandom as its predecessor.

However, even as its successes mounted, grumbling could be heard in the ranks. If you listened, you would hear it in conventions, it was stated in some reviews (usually those published in magazines less dependent on studio good will for their survival), and it was even mentioned by two speakers at the Smithsonian Institution's 1992 symposium on STAR TREK. The source of the malcontent? "Frankly," it was said, "the characters are kind of boring."

This should come as a surprise to no one, primarily because of Roddenberry's guiding vision. Gene Roddenberry notoriously worked hard to make a universe in which mankind's worst mistakes were dispatched and long forgotten. For example, when Harlan Ellison submitted his original script for "City On The Edge Of Forever," it included a crewman addicted to drugs. The script was altered to remove the addicting reference as well as that character altogether. Roddenberry asserted that by the 23rd century, "those problems would have been solved." Similarly, in THE NEXT GENERATION, the new Enterprise has an on-board bar—which doesn't serve alcohol. It serves synthohol, a synthetic alcohol substitute (hence the name) without the negative side-effects.

It's difficult if not impossible to blame Roddenberry for envisioning a world without war, inequality or fear. Isn't that dream part of what attracted us all to STAR TREK in the first place? The problem is, perfection makes for bad drama. Dramatic situations involve conflict, but conflict is not found in perfection.

Conflict is often divided into three classes: man vs. man, man vs. nature, and man vs. himself. It is in this latest category that THE NEXT GENERATION finds itself most deficient, particularly when one considers the case of sustained inner conflict—ongoing conflict within an individual.

## WHERE'S THE INNER CONFLICT?

THE NEXT GENERATION is sorely lacking sustained inner conflict. While characters occasionally experience inner conflict, it is usually resolved at the end of the episode. Will Riker experienced momentary inner conflict in "The Best of Both Worlds" when he was forced to consider that he might have to take permanent command of the Enterprise. Beverly Crusher has had at least two difficult romantic entanglements—she has passed on both by the end of each respective episode. Geordi rarely has any inner conflict, and none of it is sustained.

The list continues, with perhaps the worst case being Data. He not only has no conflict, but is repeatedly presented as incapable of experiencing emotion. If conflict is defined as the difference between what a character is or has and what that character desires or desires to be, Data can be considered to be conflict-less.

On the other hand, the original Trek was filled with sustained inner conflict. Indeed, it was one of the dramatic engines that kept the series moving. In many episodes Kirk's fear of losing command of his Enterprise plays an integral part in the storyline. Likewise, another recurring theme is Spock's deep-seated anxiety that he is not "Vulcan" enough. McCoy is concerned that mankind is becoming less humane and more technological, leading to (among other things) his apprehension over the Transporter.

What few imperfections or vices we see in the crew of the new Enterprise are really little more than quirks. Deanna Troi, for example, is a chocolate fanatic. But we know that she works out with Beverly Crusher, so we can overlook her quirk, and even sympathize with her. Will Riker fell in love with a hologram in "11001001," but she was programmed to be as appealing as possible so we are again able to overlook his imperfection.

Non-regular characters are allowed to have imperfections, and have proven quite popular because they open up dramatic possibilities that were closed to the regular characters. Barclay, the holo addict from "Hollow Pursuits," was popular enough to bring back in another episode in the following season. Gowron, who first appeared in "Reunion" (the K'Ehleyr episode), has proved to be something of a back-stabber . While this is behavior to be expected of a Klingon, it would never be tolerated in Worf.

The regular characters can take part in serious imperfection, but only if their actions are beyond their control. Picard is ready to leave the Enterprise to its own devices in "Lonely Among Us," and in back to back episodes Troi is taken over by hostile aliens. There will be no analogy in THE NEXT GENERATION to Spock commandeering the Enterprise in order to save his previous Captain. THE NEXT GENERATION characters have more in common with Dr. Richard Kimball, AKA The Fugitive: predictably, Kimball would stop to help any injured bystander, no matter how close behind Lieutenant Girard may have been.

# SPLIT PERSONALITIES

Aside from the lack of personal failings, another major reason behind the relative lack of conflict when comparing THE NEXT GENERATION to the original STAR TREK is split-personality. In the twenty years between the two, many roles in the original were split into two roles for THE NEXT GENERATION. This "split-personality syndrome" has the effect of limiting dramatic possibilities.

As an example, consider James T. Kirk, the brash, somewhat egotistical womanizer of the sixties Trek. He is the youngest man to have achieved the command of a starship in the history of Starfleet, a fact which is always on the periphery of his consciousness. He has a reputation to live up to, and he often puts off personal pleasure for the good of his career.

In THE NEXT GENERATION, the strong commanding officer character has been split into two components. One component retains the respect and exceptional command abilities that characterized Kirk as a command figure; this is Jean-Luc Picard. The other component, Will Riker, retains Kirk's convivial personality and his penchant for sexual conquests.

This may seem like a trivialization, but it lies at the core of character-driven drama. Characters with conflicting values have a high potential for drama. Characters who are more one-dimensional lack much of this potential. Spock stealing the Enterprise, driven by loyalty to his former Captain, committing mutiny against his current Captain and friend, has a high dramatic value, as does Kirk's fear of losing his ship. Riker will never steal his Enterprise, and Picard is calmly and completely in control of his ship. This may make Picard an admirable man, and the kind of person we'd like to see in charge of the tremendous power that is a starship, but it limits dramatic possibilities. Having Kirk fear the loss of his command is dramatically viable. Having Picard calmly in control is dull.

The medical care character follows the same pattern. In the original series, Dr. Leonard McCoy was both physician and psychiatrist, able to care for the mind and the body, and called upon to counsel as often as to heal.

In THE NEXT GENERATION, this character is also split into two parts. One part, Counselor Deanna Troi, would seem to be a natural for dramatic possibilities, although it took the production staff and writers the better part of a season to determine how to use her effectively. The other part, Doctor Crusher, separated from the mental/emotional aspect of McCoy, is often dramatically restricted, limited to physically caring for sick and injured characters and often kept away from the real action of the story. Troi counsels the Captain, while Crusher heals the casualties.

Perhaps the worst split is Spock. In THE NEXT GENERATION, he has been delineated in no less than four characters—the Outsider (Data, Worf), the First Officer (Riker), and the Science specialist (Data, Wesley). Many of these characters have been left too one-dimensional. Although the combined skills of the actors and the writers have overcome many of the shortcomings that were evident in the first season, dramatic possibilities are severely limited.

Worf, for example, is used more often as a tool to show how tough a particular alien or alien-possessed crew member truly is, rather than as an ambassador of an alien race or a trained security expert.

Data is left as the weakest of the lot. Often portrayed as being completely unable to feel, it is his wish (and the fine line between a wish and a desire is never fully explained) to experience what it is to be human. As an individual incapable of feeling, Data is without dramatic possibilities. It is significant that all of the episodes featuring Data that have been popular also feature a strong hint at his possibly being able to feel, but not realizing it. This is the only way to inject drama into this character.

A side effect of the many character splits is that THE NEXT GENERATION was initially burdened with far too many characters. THE NEXT GENERATION was envisioned as an ensemble cast without stars as such, but with nine leads, it was top-heavy in the first season. It was difficult to find something for everyone to do, and many characters had overlapping responsibilities.

# FAMILY CONFLICT

There is one vast arena for potential drama that THE NEXT GENERATION has tapped, albeit in self-contained, isolated instances. This is the conflict between members of the family. After careful inspection, it seems that Starfleet recruits the majority of its members from broken and/or dysfunctional homes.

Jean-Luc Picard had a poor relationship with his brother. They vied constantly for the affection and attention of their father. This conflict has strained their relationship for most of their lives, and only after the events of "Best of Both Worlds" and "Family" do they come to a better understanding and respect for one another. (It is worth mentioning that, as happy as we are that the brothers Picard are somewhat reunited, possibilities for future conflict were limited by the decision to end their conflict.)

William Riker has had a similarly strained relationship with his father. He harbors intense resentment for his father for having separated from his mother and for having been away from him so often during his youth. After his father comes on board the Enterprise, they come to an understanding of one another by attempting to beat out each other's brains. Again, although they avoided patricide in the reconciliation, dramatic possibilities were shunted aside.

Once more the list continues. Beverly Crusher lost her husband; Wesley Crusher lost his father. An early hint that either might in the least resent Picard subconsciously for leading the Away Team in which he was lost was dashed before it could congeal into solid drama. Tasha Yar apparently had no family of whom she was aware, other than her sister; the state of their relationship as of Tasha's departure is somewhat ambiguous.

Deanna Troi's relationship with her mother is comically strained. Worf's real parents are dead and, having found one another, he and his brother take some time to readjust to one another's presence. And again, there is Data, who found his father/creator after believing him to be dead, only to have him die within a few hours (Shakespeare would be proud). And in an earlier episode, Data found, previously unknown to him, an "evil" twin brother; they were almost immediately estranged and at odds.

# CHANGING TIMES AND THE PRIME DIRECTIVE

A final problem with developing conflict on THE NEXT GENERATION lies not with the writers, not with the production crew, but rather with the times. If STAR TREK was a function of the sixties, with its references to Vietnam, hippies and the Cold War, THE NEXT GENERATION is a function of the nineties, and is very concerned with political correctness, often represented by the Prime Directive.

The Prime Directive now fulfills the mission for which it was originally intended. It keeps Starfleet (or, in other words, Riker and Picard) from interfering in the development of alien cultures. Occasionally this has been handled suitably, resulting in a thought-provoking episode such as "Who's Watching the Watchers," in which Picard is mistaken for the God of an alien culture. More often the Prime Directive has worked poorly (in a dramatic sense), as in "Justice," in which Picard pleads to a mostly unseen and unheard planetary deity for the life of Wesley Crusher, who has unknowingly broken a local law by disturbing some flowers.

When the Prime Directive doesn't work, it is usually because it is used to justify inaction on the part of one or more characters. That this happens so often is due in part to the fandom joke that Kirk never managed not to break the Prime Directive in his exploits. It is important to note, however, that the original series writers had Kirk ignore the Prime Directive because it was dramatically wise for them to do so. Sensing the dramatic potential in both Kirk's actions, and in conflict between Kirk and Starfleet/the Federation, they wrote accordingly. In THE NEXT GENERATION, the Prime Directive is too often an excuse to keep characters indecisive, and dramatically dull.

None of this is to say that THE NEXT GENERATION or its characters are not worth enjoying. Rarely does any program survive for six seasons without some worthwhile qualities. THE NEXT GENERATION did not get to be at the top of its pile without providing some truly first rate entertainment. It is also worth noting that all of us have been watching and enjoying the program (as of this writing) for five years. Still, it's interesting to speculate on what might have occurred if just one unpredictable, unfathomable character had been included. Instead of six seasons, the dramatic possibilities might have been endless.

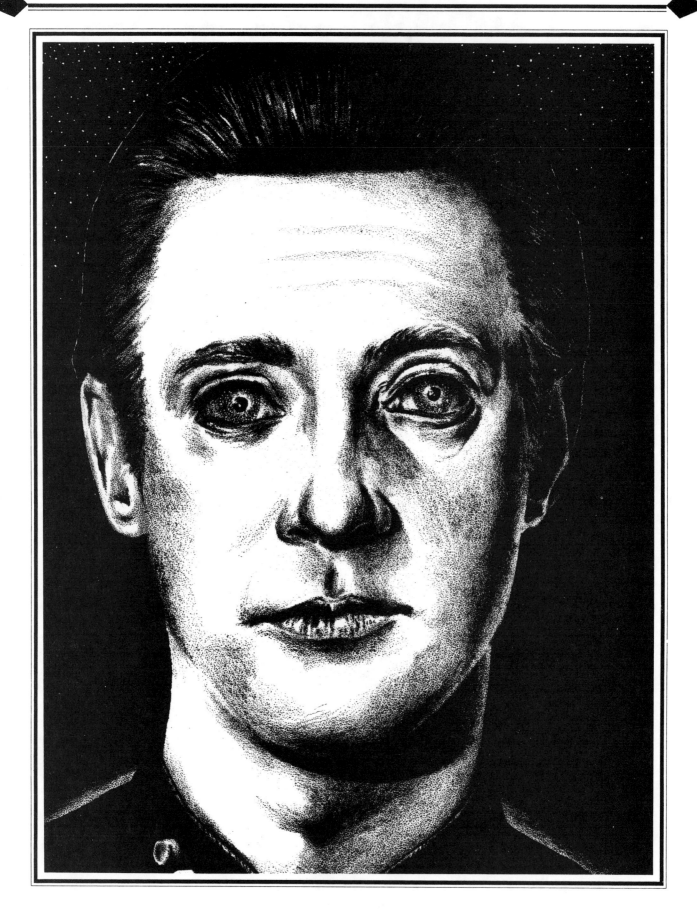

# DATA
# THE VERY SPECIAL ANDROID

> *At first Data was criticized as being just a Mr. Spock knock-off, but the character has emerged as much more than that. In many ways, though, he has captured the interest of viewers in ways Mr. Spock was did back in the sixties.*

**by K. Joyce McDonald and Richard Heim Jr.**

# THE IRREPRESSIBLEANDROID

by K. Joyce McDonald

*"... the man-machine ambiguity is emphasized by making the two physically indistinguishable so that robots became not just an external enemy but a fifth column within the human ranks."—Igor Aleksander and Piers* Burnett, REINVENTING MAN

## OUR AFFECTION FOR ANDROIDS

I am sitting at a 1984 IBM PC which I have christened HAL. My toaster has no name. If the house were to catch fire, my family knows that after they were safe, I would rush back in to save HAL. The children also know that when they set fire to my last toaster, I shed not a tear. Why?

Return for a moment to the voyages of Captain Kirk's Enterprise. Did you secretly wish that Kirk had afforded Roger Korby and his androids a little more respect? Did you hope that Spock carefully catalogued the remaining knowledge of the OLD ONES? Did you hope very much that Flint immediately set about creating another Rayna as soon as Kirk was out of sight? Did you feel some regret at the destruction of VAAL? In other words, did you feel that computers and androids serve better as friends than enemies?

We tend to anthropomorphise robots, calling them "he" or "she," and ascribing them human characteristics. We have always had a love affair with machines. Robots, especially androids, reflect our own image, which seals the emotional bond.

Our affections, however, are tinged with fear since, like Dr. Frankenstein, we cannot predict the outcome of our creations. Could fear have been the source of Kirk's antipathy? Fear certainly tinged his affection for Rayna.

Fear and affection figure into the future predictions of today's roboticists. Most roboticists agree that the human/robot distinction will become so blurred that laws may require that androids be colored blue for easy recognition. Imagine Data standing on the bridge singing, "Am I Blue?" At least Data's gold is more palatable than blue, but could this be the reason why Dr. Soong did not give him flesh tones? We are delighted to welcome him into the human race, but aren't we glad Lore couldn't pass for human?

University of Minnesota cultural anthropologist, Arthur Harkins, is already working on an android civil rights bill to protect our new robotic citizens. Harkins once predicted that before the year 2000, the first test case of a human-robot marriage will be in the courts. This prediction was made several years ago. Assessing the current state of robot development, his prediction seems highly unlikely. Still, I find HAL a much better companion than many of my human acquaintances.

The two STAR TREK's are an interesting study in contrasts, thanks primarily to our special android Data and the enlightened Captain Picard. Kirk's modus operandi was "machines are confusing and unpredictable—perhaps we are better off without them." Picard's is "Yes, they are even dangerous, but our job is to correct the mistakes and reap the benefits of their contributions." Perhaps the differing philosophies of the two captains reflect the advances that humans have made in the area of computers and robotics, as well as our increased tolerance and understanding of beings different from ourselves.

## HISTORIC AND LITERARY ROBOT PROTOTYPES

Isaac Asimov gave the world its modern concept of the robot. In stories written in the forties, and collected in 1950 in the book I, ROBOT, Asimov refuted the dim and gloomy views of Karl Capek (in "R.U.R.," a play) and Fritz Lang (METROPOLIS, a 1926 motion picture).

While Asimov is credited with inventing the Three Laws of Robotics, he was always quick to point out that they were actually invented by writer/editor John W. Campbell in the mid-forties. Campbell derived them from the robots Asimov had written about and insisted that they were implicit in what Asimov had already written. But while it was Campbell who coined the three laws themselves, today everyone knows them as "Asimov's Three Laws of Robotics." One of the places these were set down is in Asimov's 1954 novel THE CAVES OF STEEL. They are:

1) A robot may not injure a human being, or through inaction allow a human being to come to harm.

2) A robot must obey the orders given it by human beings except where such orders would conflict with the First law.

3) A robot must protect its own existence as long as such protection does not conflict with the First or Second Law.

While some people have incorrectly maintained that all science fiction robots must adhere to these laws, this is not so. Even Isaac Asimov has written stories demonstrating how a robot can exist missing one or more of the laws, and what the result would be. Such stories even appear in the seminal book I, ROBOT.

In his 1985 book ROBOTICS, Marvin Minsky (one of the world's leading authorities on artificial intelligence) states that Asimov introduced the term "robotics," but had no clear concept of how robots would actually be built. In describing a robot brain, the term "electronic" should replace "positronic." (The positron was discovered in 1932 and is defined as a negative electron.)

## FOOD FOR THOUGHT

Part of the fun of this study is to discover if Data's existence is actually possible. Let's look at a few of his capabilities and see what historical background robotics can offer. (By the way, "android" is the term for a robot built in the form of a man. A robot approximating a human female should be called a "gynoid," a cow would be a "bovoid," etc.)

1) Data can eat and drink.

Jaques de Vaucanson created a duck which could eat, drink, simulate digestion, and excrete. Displayed first in 1738, it caused great amazement when it drank three glasses of wine.

2) Data can play the violin.

The same Vaucanson created an android flutist that became the first mechanical device to excel over most people at the performance of a learned skill.

3) Data can make love.

Humans are quite creative in their development of sex toys, but perhaps Data's "functionality" has a nobler purpose. If he is a repository for the colonists' knowledge, could he not also carry their genetic material, i.e., a sperm bank?

# SNEEZING AND WHISTLING AND OTHER ANDROID MOTOR SKILLS

During our evolution, our physical capabilities were quite advanced before we developed any high-level mental capabilities. Why, then, have we developed computers capable of making complicated medical diagnoses or performing complex mathematics when we are struggling to program a robot to follow a sidewalk? (Indeed, Carnegie Mellon's Artificial Intelligence lab took 10,000 lines of code to accomplish such a task.)

Computers mirror man's accomplishments. Like a mirror, computer evolution is the reverse of man's. Why mentality first, then motor skills?

For higher-level thinking (such as writing literature or performing mathematical calculations), we must develop an algorithm: a plan for performing these tasks.

In developing our physical capabilities, we have had to rely more on practice, practice, practice. Although physical movements can be taught to some extent (such as dance or sports), humans usually rely on subconscious mental instructions to our muscles. Talent for certain physical activities also appear to be inborn (such as Baryshnikov's flair for dance, or Michael Jordan's ability to fly).

Because they are on a subconscious level, we can't really say how our brains work during physical activities. Until we do understand the algorithms for physical activities, we can't properly program robots or androids to re-create them.

Data's actions have shown us that even Soong (his creator) couldn't program him for everything. He had to sacrifice some motor abilities in favor of others. Data can't sneeze or whistle properly because he has very little need for these attributes.

Sung did, however, give him the capability to self-program any capabilities he lacked. In "The Big Goodbye," was he able to tie his own shoes? In "The Naked Now" were his "multiple techniques" and "wide variety of pleasuring" original or self-programmed? (If the latter is true, then this is some promiscuous android. If he's pre-programmed, no wonder Soong had no memory space left for whistling).

"The Schizoid Man" showed us how well Data is programmed for physical activity. Recall that Grandpa Graves shut Data off and superimposed his own neurological information on the android's brain. Under Graves' control, Data's body could now whistle, but his physical movements were sometimes clumsy as reflected by an odd skip to his walk. Failure to make physical adjustments proved to be Graves' downfall. Unable to control Data's strength, Graves turned the android, who is noted for his gentleness, into a potentially lethal adversary.

Viewing Graves and Lore as androids proves that Soong's programming priorities for Data were in the right place. Remember when Data was stuck in a Chinese Finger Puzzle ("Last Outpost")? Here, Data's own mental priorities chose chastisement and humiliation over the easier route: He could have easily ripped the puzzle apart and tossed it aside.

## THE HIGH-TECH CONCEPT OF "DOWNLOADING"

*"And if it should ever become possible to transfer human    consciousness into an android body. . . I do not know if, having once been human, a person could adapt."*

—Data in Jean Lorrah's *Survivors.*

Grant Fjermedal in THE TOMORROW MAKERS tells of an astounding method for programming the electronic brain called "Downloading." Hans Moravec of Carnegie-Mellon University's Autonomous Mobile Robot Laboratory wrote a paper called "Robots That Rove" which describes the transfer of information from a human brain to a computerized brain. The computerized brain can then be duplicated, the copies being placed in robotic bodies which essentially guarantee immortality to the owner of the human brain. Moravec has hopes that this procedure will be developed within his lifetime so that he can take advantage of it.

Moravec's process sounds like what was used in "What Are Little Girls Made Of?" to androidize Roger Korby, his assistant and Kirk. Dr. Richard Daystrom used some type of downloading process in "The Ultimate Computer" to impress his mental engrams upon the M-5 computer. In "The Schizoid Man," Dr. Graves accomplished this by an unknown process after shutting Data off. In real life, however, the transfer will be performed by an accomplished surgeon with the help of holographic and magnetic resonance equipment.

While not technically satisfying, "The Schizoid Man" did deal with some interesting outcomes. It emphasized that getting used to an android's body will take some practice (Data/Graves had a strange skip to his walk and could not control Data's strength). Another important point is that downloading an insane mind will only make for an insane android. But don't watch this episode for its technical virtues—watch it to see what Brent does to rescue a script which is schizoid itself.

## A REAL LIFE EXPERIENCE WITH "CONTAGION"

One of my favorite episodes of ST—TNG is "Contagion." Primarily because it is technically and aesthetically satisfying. After spending four months teaching in a lab with approximately fifty personal computers going at once, I have begun to appreciate its significance even more.

Early in my DOS class (That's Disk Operating System), we were formatting disks when a message began flashing on several screens: "Red State! Germ offensing—Aircop." Such was my real-world introduction to computer viruses. And I knew practically zilch about viruses in general, much less what to do about the ones staring my students in the face.

A couple of afternoons in university libraries yielded very little information that I didn't already know. Most of the articles I found dealt with the sensational invasion of ArpaNet by a high government official's son. I was more interested in what to do about Aircop, and even more important, what Aircop was going to do to us. Unfortunately, the other computer instructors were just as lost as I was.

We did have some symptoms to investigate, however. Occasionally, a disk drive would start running without warning and a disk would end up wiped clean. The students soon realized the value of backing up their data.

A file directory of a disk would produce a list of file names full of strange non-English characters. Because the file names now contained non-English characters, no program would recognize or allow us to access that file in any way. That means we couldn't copy the file, print it, edit it or even look at it. Students therefore lost a lot of files.

If we tried to print from the screen the listing of garbled file names, the printer would print erratically, sometimes printing fat characters, sometimes thin characters, sometimes in-between. Sometimes the printer would print the words in columns running down the page rather than across.

What does all this mean? First, it indicates how helpless most of us are (including experienced programmers) in the face of virus infestation. Unlike those in "Contagion," these viruses are not produced by ancient aliens. They are produced by our fellow human beings. Second, as in "Contagion," virus infestation can cause the computer to perform in a completely unpredictable manner. Part of the cure has to be determining whether the unpredictable behavior is an unanticipated result of using the software in a new way, or if it is indeed caused by a virus invasion.

In its optimism, ST—TNG concludes that the most advanced cybernetic construct in existence, AKA Data, will be able to diagnose and cure the virus himself. Until then, computer professionals will have to study and experiment with human-created cures until we have anticipated every possible virus behavior, or until humans quit creating viruses. Of course, by then, computers themselves may be capable of creating their own viruses!

**Bibliography**

Asimov, Isaac, I, Robot. New York: Ballantine Books, 1950

Minsky, Marvin, Robotics. Garden City, NY: Anchor Press/Doubleday, 1985

Fjermedal, Grant. THE TOMORROW MAKERS; Brave New World of Living-Brain Machine. New York: McMillan, 1986

Regis, Ed, "Roboticist Hans Moravec," OMNI, August 1989.

# DID DATA PULL THE TRIGGER?

by Richard Heim Jr.

In the ST-TNG episode "The Most Toys," trader Kivas Fajo kidnaps Data in order to make him part of his "collection." We learn that Fajo is somewhat like Harry Mudd, except that he is evil, uncaring, selfish, immoral, unprincipled, greedy and ruthlessly criminal. Fajo also demonstrates that he is a cold-blooded killer when he murders Varria during the escape attempt Varria and Data make.

The trader drops his Veron T disrupter, shocked at what he has done. Data seizes the moment, picks up the disrupter and attempts to take Fajo into custody. Fajo refuses to surrender and taunts Data, threatening to kill others if Data does not acquiesce. Data takes aim at Fajo. But just then the android is caught in the Enterprise's Transporter beam. We *don't know* whether Data pulled the trigger or would have pulled it—we are not allowed to witness the event.

Back on the Enterprise, O'Brien, before materializing Data, notes that the weapon "seems to have discharged." He deactivates it, then completes the materialization. When Riker confronts Data with the fact that the disrupter was in a state of discharge, Data does not outright deny firing it, he only suggests that "perhaps something occurred during transport." Riker finds that explanation a little hard to swallow, and so do I.

Although we will probably never know for sure, I find myself wondering: Did the disrupter really discharge due to transport, or did Data actually pull the trigger? It is my contention that the writers and producers of ST—TNG have, over the last three seasons, given us enough data about Data to formulate a reasonable answer to this question.

The first step in answering the question is to determine if Data *could have* pulled the trigger. Is Data physically capable of experiencing the emotions that would prompt him to kill? This can be stated another way: Data is an android with a positronic brain. Is such an android capable of feeling emotions? The answer is an unqualified yes.

In the episode "Datalore," Data's android brother, Lore, was certainly emotional. Dr. Noonian Soong made Lore perfect, "so completely human that the colonists became envious of him. Dr. Soong gave him "the full richness of human needs and ambitions." Lore understood humor, enjoyed pleasing humans (as long as it served his needs), was sarcastic, deceptive, treacherous, contemptuous, arrogant and mercilessly violent. With his emotional positronic brain, Lore brought about the death of 411 colonists and nearly killed the entire Enterprise crew.

Another example of an emotional android with a positronic brain is Lal ("The Offspring"). Lal's positronic brain was similar to Data's. It was programmed by Data using a new submicron matrix transfer technology, and was initialized using neural transfers from Data's brain. After the transfers were completed, Lal possessed the sum of Data's programming. When Lal began using verbal contractions, a skill Data's program hadn't mastered, he realized she had exceeded his abilities.

With Lal's passage into sentience, she began to feel emotions. She felt affection toward Data and expressed it with an action she had observed in humans—by holding Data's hand. Near the end, Lal felt love for Data. After her interview with Admiral Haftel, Lal felt confusion and fear. The fear manifested itself physically as a discomfort in her chest or abdomen. Unfortunately, Lal's positronic brain was not identical to Data's—there were "variations on the quantum level." Emotional awareness, for her, was a malfunction—a symptom of cascade failure in her neural net system. Emotions caused her destruction.

These two examples demonstrate that an android with a positronic brain is *capable* of feeling emotions. Then why doesn't Data?

The answer to that question must lie in Data's programming. Lore noted that, after their experience with him, "the colonists petitioned Soong to make a more comfortable, less perfect android." That android was Data. As a less perfect model, Data admits that he is "quite deficient in some human information." For example, he doesn't understand humor, can't speak in contractions, and finds certain human characteristics (such as sneezing) interesting.

Data is impartial: He relates facts and information as accurately and truthfully as he can. He "follows protocol to the letter" ("The Most Toys"). Most importantly to Data, he can't feel emotions: "I have no feelings of any kind" ("The Ensigns of Command"). It is clear that Dr. Soong completely programmed emotions out of Data.

However, this is not the whole story. Data has the ability to learn, to understand and to cope with new situations ("The Measure of a Man"). In response to Data's query, "Is not honesty always the preferred choice?" Picard replies, "Excessive honesty can be disastrous, particularly in a commander. Knowing your own limitations is one thing. Advertising them to your crew can damage your credibility as a leader." ("The Ensigns of Command".) Here Data learns that withholding information may sometimes be necessary.

In this same episode, when Ard'rian suggests that Data may need to use reverse psychology to accomplish his mission, he learns deception. Data's concert performance demonstrates to Picard that Data has learned to be creative. In "The Measure of a Man," Data packs his Starfleet medals (because "I just wanted them"), a book from Picard (he valued it because it reminded him of friendship), and a holographic portrait of Yar (because "she was special to me").

Data is uncomfortable discussing certain aspects of his duplicate ("Datalore"). He acts very mysterious, secretive and cautious while he was constructing Lal ("The Offspring"). Dr. Crusher finds it hard to believe that Data is incapable of giving Lal love. To her, his *actions* demonstrate his love, even if he can't *feel* the emotion. When Lal dies, Data incorporates her programs into his own, thereby transferring her memories to himself.

He is now able to access the emotional experiences of an android with a positronic brain because they are a part of him. From the foregoing it is clear that, while Data may not be able to *feel* emotions, his actions sometimes *demonstrate* emotions. Dr. Soong may have programmed out emotions from Data, but the desire to be human remained in his programming (either by accident or by design). At this point, I can say the evidence supports the statement that Data could have acted in an emotional way and fired the disrupter.

However, for the sake of argument, let's say Data is devoid of emotions and will not learn to respond in an emotional way. Then what governs his actions? As he explained to trader Fajo, Data was "designed with a fundamental respect for life in all its forms and a strong inhibition against causing harm to living beings." (Note: Only a strong *inhibition*, *not* a prohibition.) Data is "programmed with the ability to use deadly force in the cause of defense. But I would not participate in a murder."

Data's programmed respect for life leads him to take whatever action is necessary to protect life: he saved Varria's life by sitting in the chair. This respect for life is also evident in references made in "Datalore." La-Forge called Dr. Soong "Earth's foremost robotic scientist" who, according to Yar, "tried to make Asimov's dream of a positronic brain come true." In their deference to Isaac Asimov, the writers are undoubtedly acknowledging him, for legal purposes, as the originator of the concept of the positronic brain.

There are hidden implications in this. With the concept of the positronic brain come the Asimovian Laws of Robotics These three laws were programmed into the robots by their creators. A Zeroth Law was formulated by the two most famous Asimov robots, R. Giskard and R. Daneel: A robot may not injure humanity or, through inaction, allow humanity to come to harm (FOUNDATION AND EARTH, pages 346-347). Obviously, these laws were not directly incorporated into the Roddenberry universe. Lore, a "perfect" android, lived only by the third law and ignored the rest. Data's fundamental respect for living creatures, on the other hand, reflects these Asimovian concepts, but he is not necessarily governed by them.

An unemotional Data with the ability to learn, who is also programmed with a fundamental respect for life, may make rational decisions that appear to mimic emotion. According to Picard, "Lal" in Hindi means "beloved." Did Data name his offspring "Beloved" because he loved her, or did he make the logical decision that, based on what he had read about human parenting, "Beloved" would be an appropriate name for a child?

In "The Ensigns of Command," Data kissed Ard'rian, not because he felt like it, but because he logically reasoned that she "appeared to need it." He saw that she was unhappy and did what he concluded would make her feel better (based on what he learned from her earlier about kissing).

The preceding provides the basis for the following scenario. When Data tries to take Fajo into custody, the trader refuses to surrender. Fajo taunts Data: "If only you could feel rage over Varria's death, feel the need for revenge, then maybe you could fire. But you're just an android. You can't feel anything, can you? It's just another interesting intellectual puzzle for you. Another of life's curiosities." The taunts don't upset Data, for he *can't* be upset. The murder of Varria is not, in itself, enough to cause Data to take deadly action against Fajo. *The key event in this confrontation is*

*threat to kill more people if Data does not acquiesce.*

Killing is nothing to Fajo. He has killed; if he says he will kill again, then he undoubtedly will carry out his threat. His taunts reinforce this conclusion. Data's fundamental respect for life and strong inhibition against causing harm to living beings lead him to this decision: he cannot allow Fajo to cause harm to any more living beings. I believe this is what Data means when he says, "I cannot permit this to continue."

Fajo gives Data two choices: acquiesce or fire. Data concludes that his acquiescence would be no guarantee that Fajo would not kill again. The trader makes a crucial mistake when he assumes Data would not murder him. Data logically concludes that the only way to protect living beings against Fajo is to kill him—not murder a human being, but rather execute a murderer. Hence he takes aim and, just as the Transporter beam grabs him, pulls the trigger.

He does not admit to pulling the trigger because Riker does not directly ask him if he pulled the trigger. Riker states only that the weapon was in a state of discharge. Data does not confess to pulling the trigger because, as Picard had said, "excessive honesty can be disastrous."

Did Data pull the trigger? I say yes, logically or emotionally, either way. Do you think I'm right? Probably only one person knows for certain, and he may not even have decided yet! Perhaps he wants us, the viewers, to decide?

# GUINAN & PICARD WHO WERE THEY?

> *Many fictional characters have historical origins. This is the case with two of the more colorful crew members of THE NEXT GENERATION.*

**by Kay Doty**

# SHARED PAST?

Ⓞne of the most intriguing mysteries surrounding STAR TREK: THE NEXT GENERATION is the relationship between Captain Picard and Guinan. Occasionally, one of the other makes a comment indicating they share a past. This adds to the mystique, but does nothing to solve the mystery.

During interviews, Paramount has stated that this secret will never be revealed. Never is a long time, but not knowing the answer to this minor mystery is part of the fun of the show. Fans and writers are left to speculate. . . what was their past relationship?

While the answer to that may be a long time in coming, hints were dropped in the episode "Time's Arrow" (Part One), the fifth season finale/cliffhanger. One thing we do know, in real life, a woman bar-tender named Guinan, and a space adventurer named Piccard, made unrelated world-wide headlines on the same spring day back in May, 1931.

Fiction writers, TV producers, playwrights and storytellers look in many places for just the right names for their characters. Some of their sources include their families, newspapers (obituary pages are great), books, and the pages of history. One can only speculate that the names of Guinan and Picard were suggested by the people involved in those two true 1931 events.

## "Balloonists Reach Safety After Trip 52,500 Feet In Air!"

This and similar headlines, datelined May 29, 1931 Gurgl, Tyrol, Austria, screamed the success of Professor Auguste Piccard's dream of: ". . . becoming the Columbus of the stratosphere." Accompanied by Dr. Charles Kipfer, the two scientists' successful 17 hour flight was made in a hermetically sealed gondola (called a car at the time) attached to a hydrogen-filled balloon. The pressurized gondola was built from a design Auguste and his brother Jean built in 1905 for use in deep sea exploration.

The flight began May 27 in Augsburg, Germany and ended May 28 on the Gurgl glacier in Austria. The pair spent a comfortable night high in the Tyrolese Alps and were assisted down the glacier by would-be rescuers. Identical twins, Auguste Antoine and Jean Felix Piccard were born January 28, 1884 in Basle, Switzerland into a family of scientists and inventors. As children, they developed an interest in scientific exploration after reading Jules Verne's TWENTY THOUSAND LEAGUES UNDER THE SEA.

After Auguste's famous flight into the Austrian stratosphere, the pair continued their scientific studies Jean's interest remaining in the atmosphere while Auguste returned to his work on the bathyscaph for underwater exploration. He made an unsuccessful attempt to descend to the ocean floor in 1948, but refused to be stopped by failure.

Going back to the drawing board, Auguste built another vehicle, the Triest. In 1953, he and his son Jacques descended to a depth of 10,168 feet in the Mediterranean Sea. Jacques later set a submarine record (at the time) by descending to a depth of 35,800 feet in the Pacific Ocean Mariana Trench. Auguste continued his science studies until his death in 1962.

Jean went to work adding improvements to the balloon, and in 1934 he and his wife Jeannett Ridlon Piccard (also a scientist) broke Auguste's record by soaring 57,559 feet into the stratosphere.

After Jean's death in 1963, Jeannette (Ridlon) Piccard, the first woman to fly into the stratosphere by means of a balloon, became a consultant to the National Aeronautics and Space Administration (NASA). The contributions made by the Piccard family to the world's attempt to conquer space are incalculable.

## "'Tex' Guinan Happy to Arrive in London."

This much smaller headline can also be found in newspapers dated May 29, 1931, but it didn't cause much of a stir; that came the following day. Billed as "Texas Guinan, New York's nightclub queen," the former actress was the owner of several speak-easys during the prohibition era (1920-1933). The Volstead Act became the eighteenth amendment, better known as the Prohibition Act, when three-fourths of the states ratified the bill on January 16, 1919. The law went into effect exactly one year later on January 16, 1920. Eventually every state but Connecticut and Rhode Island ratified the bill which would not be repealed until February 20, 1933.

Millions of Americans were unwilling to give up their drinking habits, thus giving birth to the type of establishments owned and operated by "Texas" Guinan. Most were private clubs, but all were called "speakeasys." Many small time hoodlums such as Al Capone were also spawned as a result of the Prohibition Act. They tried to control the importation of Illegal beverages, and for the most part succeeded, becoming rich in the process. In Guinan they were not completely successful, for beneath the glitzy exterior, she was a hard-headed business woman. She had in her employ people who were just as tough as the Capones, and like Guinan, just as determined to import the desired contraband.

In addition to illegal liquor, her clubs were also known for the number of pretty "dancing girls." The turbulent twenties were just emerging from the Victorian Age, and newspapers were still reluctant to use such words as prostitute or call women anything but ladies or girls. Instead they used quotation marks to indicate that all might not be as it seemed.

Following her successful operations in New York, the flamboyant Guinan, who frequently greeted customers with, "Hello, sucker," decided to take her show on the road, so to speak. She made arrangements to present several shows at a Paris nightclub and purchased tickets to Europe on the French liner Paris for herself, her dancing girls and musicians. Her raucous aboard-ship departure party was well chronicled by the press.

Despite reports that the British home office would not allow Guinan and her troupe into the island nation, her arrival was uneventful . "I am arriving with a royal flush on my face and in my heart. I am going to keep it until I am in London for the beloved British Isles which I adore." Guinan sent this message in a telegram to a U.S. news agency upon her arrival in England.

France wasn't so hospitable. The French office of the ministry flatly refused to allow her to leave the liner Paris when it arrived at Havre, France. After hours of bickering, the troupe was permitted to disembark and take rooms in a local hotel while officials studied the legality of her contract with the Paris Nightclub.

While officials were conferring, Texas and her girls threw a wild party at the Havre hotel that endeared her to no one, except perhaps the people who attended. Officials went from referring to her entertainers as "little girls" to the less polite "Guinan's gang of girls." When immigration officials interviewed passengers on the ship, they learned that Texas and her "gang" had hosted numerous parties during the voyage from New York. A day later they issued the statement: ". . . I don't think her type of amusement is our type."

Despite a plea from an American Legion official, who cited Guinan's service as an entertainer for soldiers in France during the war (World War One), French officials refused to relent. "It's all right, suckers, we've been thrown out of better places than this," was her parting shot several days later when, after having lost all of her legal battles with the French government.

Mary Louise Cecelia (Texas) Guinan was born in Waco, Texas sometime between 1885 and 1890. Ambitious to become a vaudeville actress, she went to New York while still a teenager. Her first appearance of note was in the 1908 production of "The Gibson Girl." She also performed in night clubs, and by 1917 was appearing in silent movies and on Broadway. Guinan starred in two early sound movies, QUEEN OF THE NIGHT CLUBS in 1929 and BROADWAY THROUGH A KEYHOLE in 1933.

With the advent of prohibition, her boisterous manner made her an ideal speak-easy hostess during the turbulent 1920's. She owned and/or operated several of these "private clubs," most notably the "Texas Guinan Club," and frequently made headlines due to numerous brushes with the law during the Prohibition era.

Guinan frequently wore elaborately decorated western style clothing, decked-out her girls in silk, satin and velvet and her male musicians were dressed in tuxedos. Texas Guinan died November 5, 1933 in Vancouver, British Columbia, Canada of amoebic dysentery. Betty Hutton starred in the 1945 movie INCENDIARY BLONDE, which was based on Guinan's life.

How much of the historical Guinan and Piccard went into the mix when these characters were created for STAR TREK—THE NEXT GENERATION? Only Gene Roddenberry (an avid reader of history books), knows for sure.

# YESTERDAY'S FOES, TODAY'S ENEMIES

*Even those who complain that the regulars on THE NEXT GENERATION are too bland and chummy, agree that the one saving grace is Worf. Klingons were never nice, and even domesticated Klingons have their own way of looking at things which sometimes give humans pause. This, as well as the alien culture, has been explored to make for some very fine episodes while deepening STAR TREK as a whole.*

*When the Ferengi flopped as the new villains meant to threaten the Federation in STAR TREK—THE NEXT GENERATION, a new menace was conceived: The Borg.*

# KLINGON EPISODES

Shortly before ST-TNG debuted in the fall of 1987 it was decided to add a Klingon to the bridge crew. Originally there wasn't one anywhere in the cast. Not only doesn't the original series outline feature Worf, but the character doesn't even appear in the pilot episode, "Encounter At Farpoint." Casting Michael Dorn as the Klingon, Worf, was a last minute decision made by Gene Roddenberry. Roddenberry had earlier stated that there wouldn't be any Klingons in the new series as he'd seen the way they were used as boring standard villains in the feature films. Then the staff of TNG got an idea. What if the Federation were at peace with the Klingon empire and the Klingons were now a part of the Federation? It opened up exciting possibilities.

Worf was a wild card from the time he joined the cast. We knew little about him and weren't sure what to make of him. The character was given a chance to come into his own in episode nineteen, "Heart Of Glory." Not only did it contrast Worf with his human comrades on the Enterprise, but it also contracted Worf with the renegade Klingons whom the Enterprise rescues from a disabled vessel.

The story opens when the Enterprise receives a report of a battle in the Neutral Zone and proceeds there at Warp 7. Data locates a disabled vessel, which they identify as a Tolarian cargo ship. Life signs are detected aboard the ship but they are indistinct due to interference from the ship's engineering section. An Away Team is dispatched consisting of Geordi, Riker and Data. Geordi wears a visual acuity transmitter which sends the Enterprise images of what he is seeing.

Their investigation shows that the vessel is heavily damaged, and the three pick their way carefully through the wreckage. Geordi detects severe metal fatigue developing in the bulkhead, which will allow them only five minutes to find survivors. Data finds the compartment where the survivors were detected and forces the door open. Inside they find three Klingons, one of whom is badly hurt.

They have to get away from engineering quickly in order for the Transporter to pick them up without interference. They barely manage to escape as the ship explodes. Picard greets the Klingons, who claim they were passengers on the ship when it was attacked by the Ferengi. The three Klingons are surprised to see Worf aboard the Enterprise. After the two uninjured Klingons are taken to quarters, Picard tells Riker that he doesn't entirely believe their story.

Worf is pleased to have other Klingons to talk to, but he soon discovers that things are not all they appear to be. The other Klingons question why Worf is in the Federation and try to provoke him to learn whether or not he's a tame Klingon. Worf is not, and the Klingons, Koris and Kunivas, are pleased that Worf can display anger.

The wounded Klingon is dying so the other three go to be with him, emitting a chant when he dies. Worf joins in this in a chilling scene where the other Enterprise crew members who observe it can only watch in silent awe. They've clearly never seen anything like this before. Data later explains to Picard that the death ritual is meant to warn the dead to beware—a Klingon is on the way.

While talking to Worf, the two Klingon guests let slip that their companion's death was not in battle at the hands of an enemy. They question Worf about how he came to be in the Federation. Worf reveals that he was the sole survivor of a Romulan attack and was rescued by a human. The other Klingons reveal that they understand his solitude and confess that they are warriors without a war, fugitives who destroyed a Klingon cruiser sent to bring them back to the Klingon Empire. This puts Worf in a difficult position. Can he betray his new comrades who have declared themselves in opposition to both the Klingon Empire and the Federation?

The Enterprise detects a vessel approaching— a Klingon ship. The Klingon Captain inquires what the Enterprise is doing in the Neutral Zone. Picard explains that they have rescued some Klingons from a stricken ship. When he says who they are, the Klingon Captain reveals that Koris and the others are fugitives and requests that they be turned over to him.

Picard dispatches a security team for the Klingons. When the security team, commanded by Tasha Yar, arrives, Koris and Kunivas appeal to Worf for help. Worf seems confused. When a child runs into them and one of Klingons picks her up, Tasha thinks a hostage situation is underway, but Kunivas hands the child to Worf, explaining that Klingons do not stoop to taking hostages. They surrender willingly and are taken to a security cell. This is an interesting scene because it plays on the viewer's own prejudices towards Klingons as these aliens have always been portrayed as being one-dimensional villains—until now. Even renegade Klingons have a code of honor.

Worf learns that the Klingon ship has come to arrest Koris and Kunivas. Worf asks that he be allowed to speak to the captain of the Klingon ship. He pleads for the hostages, asking that they at least be allowed to die as warriors on a hostile world, rather than be executed while bound and helpless. The Captain admits that they are all diminished when a Klingon dies in such a manner, but he is bound to take the prisoners back with him. They pose a threat to the Klingon alliance with the Federation. In their cell, the two Klingons construct a weapon from parts cleverly secreted in their uniforms. The Klingons kill two guards while escaping but Kunivas is killed as well, leaving Koris alone.

Koris goes to Main Engineering and threatens to use his weapon to blast the dilithium crystal chamber. Worf and Picard go to engineering, and Worf talks to Koris, who pleads with him to join him as a warrior and reject the Federation. Koris urges Worf to take over the battle bridge, steal the saucer section and launch a rampage through space! Worf tells Koris that a man cannot be a warrior without duty and honor, and is finally forced to shoot and mortally wound Koris in order to save the Enterprise.

Worf goes to Koris and performs the Klingon death ritual, howling a warning as the Klingon dies. Picard and the others are strangely moved by the sight. This is a side of Worf they haven't witnessed before. Until now they'd tried to convince themselves that Worf was, under the skin, really no different from themselves. They realize now that they were wrong. A gulf of cultures separates them which they can only hope to *try* to understand.

Worf reports to the Klingon Captain that Koris and Kunivas are dead. The Captain invites Worf to join him when his tour of duty with the Enterprise is over. Worf says that he would feel honored to do so. After the Klingon ship leaves, Worf tells Picard that he was just being polite and has no real desire to leave the Enterprise. Picard replies that the bridge wouldn't be the same without him.

This one episode established Worf with more personality than all of the other characters on the Enterprise have put together. The only other one who seemed to have a background as interesting as Worf's was Tasha Yar, but her character was never properly explored. Denise Crosby chose to leave the series before the end of the first season for this very reason. Seeing the opportunity that Michael Dorn was given in "Heart Of Glory" could have only made her even more unhappy with the shallow role she had to deal with.

## TRADING PLACES

In season two the next Klingon episode turned the tables on both the series regulars as well as on the viewers. Instead of seeing a story about a Klingon aboard the Enterprise, episode 31, "A Matter Of Honor," presented us with Riker temporarily transferred to a Klingon vessel. The teleplay was by Burton Armus based on a story by Armus, Wanda M. Haight and Gregory Amos. The directing by Rob Bowman remains some of his most effective on the series.

The story opens by introducing an officer exchange program. A Benzite ensign, Mendoc, joins the Enterprise crew as part of it. When Picard mentions an opening on the Klingon ship Pagh, Riker volunteers to be the first human to serve with the Klingons. Worf helps him learn about Klingon customs: the First Officer's primary obligation, on a Klingon ship, is to kill his captain if the captain seems weak or indecisive. The Second Officer is likewise obligated to his immediate superior. Riker also prepares by sampling Klingon food in Ten Forward, much to the disgust of Pulaski and other humans. But Riker seems to enjoy it.

As Riker is about to beam over to the Pagh, Worf gives him an emergency transponder. While the two ships rendezvous, Mendoc notes a patch of microbiotic organisms on the hull of the Pagh, but says nothing: Benzite procedure requires a complete analysis before making a report. The Klingons question their new human officer, and Riker swears loyalty to the captain and the ship. When his Second Officer challenges his authority, he beats him soundly, thus winning his respect. Captain K'Argan is greatly amused by this.

The Enterprise discovers that the microbe—a subatomic bacteria that eats metal—is on its hull. At this point the Benzite mentions that he'd noticed it on the Klingon ship too. The Enterprise determines that the microbe has eaten a 12 centimeter hole in the Pagh's hull by this point, and follows the Klingon ship to warn it.

Aboard the Pagh, Riker impresses the Klingons by eating their food, but stalls when he learns that one dish he'd eaten cooked on the Enterprise is actually eaten alive by Klingons. The two Klingon women aboard express curiosity about Riker, prompting some ribald humor—Riker realizes that they have a sense of humor, even if it isn't very sophisticated, and joins in their laughter. They even discuss Klingon family matters. One Klingon is proud of his father's heroic death, while the other is ashamed that his father was once captured by Romulans, escaped, and now awaits a quiet, natural death on their homeworld.

When Riker returns to the bridge, the Captain has discovered the hole in the hull, and believes that the Enterprise is responsible. The fact that a scan beam (courtesy of Mendoc) was focused on the area for several minutes only fuels his suspicion, which he turns on Riker. Riker stands his ground; having vowed loyalty, he will serve the Pagh even in an attack on the Enterprise. When the Captain demands the Enterprise's security codes and other secrets, however, Riker refuses, since it would violate other oaths he has made. The Captain says that he would have killed Riker on the spot, as a traitor, if he had revealed those secrets. But now Riker may have the honor of dying in battle among Klingons.

Meanwhile, the Enterprise has found a means of removing the microbes, and sends a message out to the Klingons. K'Argan does not believe them, and prepares to attack. The Enterprise, unaware of this, cannot locate the cloaked vessel. K'Argan prepares to fire, and also gives this honor to Riker. Riker says he will obey, but tells the captain that his reasons are wrong, and triggers the transponder. K'Argan demands the device, which Riker yields to him.

The Enterprise locates the transponder beacon, and acts to beam Riker aboard—only to find an angry Klingon captain aboard the bridge instead. Worf subdues K'Argan and puts him under guard. Riker hails the Enterprise, as acting Captain of the Pagh, and demands the surrender of the Federation ship. Picard surrenders to Riker, and the Klingons decloak, ready to be rid of the microbe.

K'Argan returns to his ship. Riker has cleverly maintained the honor of all involved. His only short-coming, in Klingon eyes, was that he did not assassinate his superior officer. K'Argan strikes Riker a vicious blow, which Riker does not duck, thus reestablishing K'Argan's authority. Riker returns to the Enterprise, after what may have been the shortest exchange assignment on record.

## "THE EMISSARY"

Written by: Richard Manning and Hans Beimler

Directed by: Cliff Bole

The story opens with a poker game aboard the Enterprise. This routine recreation has turned up in subsequent episodes as well as it shows the main characters interacting while they're off duty. When Worf wins another poker game, he dispenses the following bit of important cultural information: Klingons never bluff.

But duty soon rears its head as the Enterprise is assigned to rendezvous with an important emissary, who is traveling at high warp speed in a stripped-down probe. When the probe is beamed aboard, the emissary proves to be a half Klingon, half human woman, K'Ehleyr. Her mission involves a Klingon ship with a crew that has been in cryonic suspension for seventy-five years. The Enterprise must try to reach them in time to delay their awakening, for they will believe that the Federation/Klingon war is still going on.

K'Ehleyr is a familiar face to Worf; she feels they have an unresolved relationship. Worf disagrees, and they argue constantly. When they meet in a holodeck battle simulation, Klingon passions are aroused (not a pretty sight), and old business soon becomes new business. Worf feels obligated to take the vow of mating, but K'Ehleyr, who is scornful of Klingon traditions, declines. Worf is very offended by this and their on-again, off-again relationship resumes its rocky course.

The Enterprise reaches the Klingon ship too late, and is attacked. A vicious battle seems imminent, until Worf has a brainstorm. He poses as the captain of the Enterprise, with K'Ehleyr his second in command, and convinces the Klingon captain that the war is over—with the Klingons as the victors. His poker playing skills save the day. What was that Worf had said about Klingons never bluffing?

This episode introduced K'Ehleyr, the lady Klingon whom Worf had once been involved with. What isn't even hinted at here is that they had a son from their previous involvement, but then Worf doesn't even know this as of yet in the series. K'Ehleyr is an interesting character who could have been developed much more. Unfortunately she'll make only one additional appearance on the series.

## THIRD SEASON EPISODES

The next Klingon episode doesn't bring back K'Ehleyr yet, but it does reveal still more about Worf's past, and in a way which is linked to the continued existence of the Klingon/Federation alliance. The third season episode "Sins Of The Father" was written by Ronald D. Moore and W. Reed Moran, based on a teleplay by Drew Deighn. Les Landau does a fine job as director, particularly in that he is required to show us the Klingon homeworld for the first time.

When the story opens, we find things in a state of ordered chaos when a Klingon exchange officer temporarily assumes Riker's duties. The officer-exchange program is now doing for the Enterprise what the Enterprise did for the Pagh in "A Matter Of Honor." The Klingon commander is harsh on his subordinates, but the over-worked crew can't help but notice that Worf is the only one escaping the Klingon's discipline.

What they fail to realize is that being polite and condescending to a fellow Klingon is a very pointed way of insulting him. At last Worf cannot stand it any longer. He is more than willing and ready to fight the visitor, only to learn that the Klingon is actually his younger brother, and that his insults were a test. Now that Worf has shown his worthiness, his brother reveals his secret: when Worf and his parents went to the outpost, which was later destroyed by the Romulans, the younger brother was left behind, presumed dead by the Empire but actually raised by another family. He has sought out Worf after all these years because their father has now been accused of helping the Romulan's notorious attack, and only the eldest son can challenge charges of treachery in the High Council. Otherwise, the stigma of a traitor will be borne by their family for seven generations. One further catch: if Worf's challenge fails, he will be executed.

Picard has Data access all the records of the massacre. The charges against Worf's father were based on the records of a recently captured Romulan vessel. Data compares these to the sensor records of the Federation ship Intrepid, which was nearby at the time, and discovers a discrepancy in the time codes. Someone has tampered with the Romulan records.

Picard and Riker accompany Worf and his brother to the Klingon home world. Worf's brother is ambushed but survives. Picard steps in as Worf's "second." The Council sessions seem to offer little hope for Worf's cause until Data also learns that another Klingon— Worf's nurse— survived the massacre as well. Picard ventures into the heart of the ancient Klingon capitol to find her, only to have her refuse her aid. On his way back he is attacked by assassins, nearly losing his life. He is saved by the old woman's change of heart, for she stabs the assassin in the back when she catches up with Picard.

Her appearance at the Council throws things into an uproar. The head of the Council calls everyone into his private chambers. The truth is revealed: the father of Worf's accuser was the real traitor. When the Romulan records were seized, this information threatened the entire power structure of the Empire, for the traitor was a member of a very ancient and powerful family. Since Worf, apparently the sole survivor of his line, was away serving in Starfleet, a decision was made to cast the blame on his father.

No one believed that he would ever challenge the charges. According to Klingon ideals, the honor of the Empire outweighs that of any single family, a point that even Worf must agree upon. It seems that he and his brother must die, until he proposes another alternative. Worf finally agrees that he will undergo discommendation, in effect "de-Klingonizing" himself, accepting the blight on his family name and exiling himself from the Empire.

Although this is humiliating, it shows true Klingon honor, for it demonstrates loyalty to the Empire and also leaves open the margin, however slight, of someday gaining revenge.

Introducing a living brother into Worf's family tree links him more directly to the Klingon Empire. Up until now he seemed to be an orphan from both. The story further emphasizes the Klingon culture and their unusual way of looking at things. The revelation of treachery by a family member of the ruling council threatens the stability of the government.

The third season also featured an important Worf subplot in the episode "The Bonding." When a woman is killed while part of an Away Team that Worf is commanding, he feels responsible. She leaves behind a young son whom Worf finally performs a Klingon ceremony with in which he takes responsibility for the boy. It's a moving episode, but unfortunately Worf's self-appointed responsibility for the boy is never mentioned again, even after Alexander, Worf's real son, comes to live aboard the Enterprise in season five.

## NEW SEASON, OLD FLAME

The fourth season episode, "Reunion," brings back Worf's old flame, K'Ehleyr. The teleplay is by Thomas Perry, Jo Perry, Ronald D. Moore and Brandon Braga. It's based on a story by Drew Deighan, Thomas Perry and Jo Perry. It features the directing of series co-star Jonathan Frakes.

As the story opens, a Klingon cruiser hails the Enterprise. Aboard it is a woman well-known to Worf. Her name is K'Ehleyr. But she isn't there to see Worf. She beams over with a message for Picard: the leader of the Klingon High Council is dying, and wants Picard to discover which of the contenders for his position has been poisoning him. K'Ehleyr also has a surprise for Worf: their encounter years before produced a son, Alexander. K'Ehleyr is now willing to make the marriage vows she earlier declined, but Worf resists because of his discommendation. He does not wish to bring shame upon her or his son.

The two Klingon contenders arrive aboard the neutral ground of the Enterprise. They are not happy to discover that Picard has been chosen by the late Klingon leader as the arbitrator who will determine the challenger's right to battle for the ascension. At the preliminary ritual, a bomb goes off, killing two Klingon aides. Picard delays further ceremonies by insisting on an archaic ritual which demands a long recitation of the challengers' accomplishments, a ritual which could take hours or days.

The Enterprise crew determines that the bomb was a sort used only by the Romulans, and that it was implanted in the forearm of the aide of one of the challengers: Worf's old enemy, the Klingon responsible for Worf's family dishonor. It seems that he, like his father, is a traitor, doing business with the Romulans.

As this goes on, K'Ehleyr tries to discover the reasons for Worf's discommendation, which neither Worf nor Captain Picard will reveal to her. She manages to put together the truth, but she is discovered and killed by the traitor. Worf discovers her body and beams over to the Klingon's ship, claiming right of revenge. His claim is questioned until he reveals that K'Ehleyr was his mate. Worf fights his enemy to the death, triumphing over him seconds before a security teams arrives to escort him back to the Enterprise. (Apparently, right of vengeance outweighs dishonor in Klingon ethics.)

The Klingon High Council approves Worf's action, since the Klingon he killed was revealed as a traitor. Picard takes him to task, but all he will receive in punishment is a reprimand on his record. Although his enemy is dead, Worf must keep the truth behind his dishonor a secret until the time is right for him and his brother to set matters straight. Worf decides that his son will be sent to Earth to be raised by his human parents, just as they raised him.

This episode annoyed a lot of fans that liked K'Ehleyr and expected to see more of her as the series continued. Having her killed off during her second appearance went down hard. Giving Worf a cute Klingon son hardly made up for it.

In the fourth season finale, "Redemption," the Klingon question once more dominates the proceedings. Written by Ronald D. Moore, the episode was directed by Cliff Bole.

As our cliff hanging adventure begins to unfold, the Enterprise is en route to the Klingon home world where Gowron is about to become the leader of the High Council. Picard asks Worf if it isn't about time that he did something about his discommendation, but Worf still feels that he must wait. Gowron's ship appears and the Klingon confers with Picard: he needs help to avert a Klingon civil war.

The family of Duras, who Worf killed awhile ago, is still very powerful. Two sisters survive Duras, and although they cannot take part in the Council, it is likely that they have something up their sleeves and they have at least three fleet commanders on their side. Picard says that he will act out his final obligations as the arbiter of succession, but cannot promise aid in any civil conflict.

Worf escorts Gowron to the Transporter room where he tells him the truth about his dishonor and asks for his help in restoring it. Gowron refuses since he would alienate the Council by revealing Duras treachery. But he is impressed by Worf nonetheless.

Worf asks Picard for a leave of absence, which is granted. Worf meets with his brother, Kurn, who feels that the Klingon leadership has betrayed the Empire and must be swept away. He is certain that Gowron will be killed by Duras' family, but promises to do it himself if not. Kurn has four squadron commanders sworn to help him. Worf, being the elder brother, chooses to change these plans. They will support Gowron, but not until he is backed into a corner by his many enemies and agrees to restore Worf's honor. Kurn agrees and talks all but one of his allies into going along with this new plan.

At the Klingon High Council, Picard asks if there are any challengers to Gowron's claim. Lursa, Duras' sister, appears with her other sister along with a Klingon boy whom they claim is the son of Duras. Under Klingon law, Picard must consider this claim as well.

At Lursa's home it is revealed that she is in collusion with the Romulans, including the shadowy commander first encountered in "The Mind's Eye." She is more patient than the Klingons, and it seems that her long-term plans may have something specifically to do with one particular human—Jean-Luc Picard.

Lursa invites Picard to her home. He beams down and she and her sister offer him tea— Earl Grey, of course. They attempt to sway him to their way of thinking. He sees through them. If he backs their claim, Gowron will certainly be killed. If he doesn't back them, they'll claim Federation interference, and start a war against Gowron.

They agree with his opinion but point out another factor—if they must fight to topple Gowron, the Federation alliance will certainly fall when they come into power. Picard leaves. The next day before the Klingon Council, Picard rejects the boy's claim because he has no experience, and back's Gowron. As predicted, the boy accuses Picard of serving Federation interests. The rest of the council backs the Duras family, leaving Gowron alone.

Later, Worf visits Gowron's ship and offers him aid in return for restoring his family's honor. Gowron scoffs, but when their ship is attacked by two other Klingon vessels, Worf takes command of the weapons station and destroys one of the attackers after tricking it into lowering its shields. Gowron's ship is at the mercy of the other attacker until Kurn's ship appears and drives them off. The Enterprise, meanwhile, has withdrawn from the battle area as Picard realizes that he cannot get involved any more deeply than he already is.

Back in the nearly empty Council hall, Gowron is sworn in as Council leader. His first act is the restoration of Worf's family honor. Worf grasps the naked blade of a Klingon dagger in the ceremony but does not flinch. They then travel to the Enterprise where Gowron again asks for Picard's help. Worf also asks, but Picard states that he cannot risk drawing the Federation into a civil war. He orders Worf to return to duty. Worf refuses and resigns his commission in Starfleet in order to join with Gowron to fight in the Klingon civil war.

As Worf is about to leave the Enterprise, Picard goes to his quarters to see him off. The entire crew lines the hallway leading to the Transporter room and they all stand at attention as he passes. Little is said (Klingons hate long good-byes) but it is obviously a moving experience for Worf.

After Worf beams off, the Enterprise leaves orbit. Down on the planet, the Duras family and their Romulan friends receive the news with some happiness. Only the boy is angry, since he is impetuous and wants to Kill Picard for passing him over. The Romulan commander, with whom the Duras family is secretly aligned, counsels patience. She's certain that Picard will be back soon enough.

It almost seems as though she has some secret reason for wanting to encounter Picard. As the episode ends, the Romulan commander steps into the light, revealing her face. She is blond, which is unusual for a Rom-

# BORG EPISODES

by Beth Wesley and James Van Hise

Maurice Hurley, the producer of ST-TNG in its early seasons, had conceived of The Borg as far back as season one. Because of poor writing, not every fan picked up on the fact that Maurice Hurley's teleplay for "Q-Who?" was actually the sequel to the cliff-hanger episode of the previous season.

The absence of the Romulans from the storyline added to the confusion, as well as the fact that "Q-Who?" leaves us with the impression that it's Q's fault that the Borg discover the existence of the Federation at all. In actuality, Q was confronting Picard and the Enterprise with the fact of the Borg's existence to show them what they'd be up against when another Borg ship entered Federation space, which would occur one year later.

The Borg are cybernetic beings, or cyborgs, ergo the name. They are part-humanoid beings with artificial intelligence incorporated into the synapses of its brain and other vital organs at birth. Bio-chips allow the Borg to inter-link with the collective memory as no one Borg is capable of singular thought. Damage to the cube-shaped Borg ship is repaired just as quickly as it occurred.

At the first encounter with the Borg, the USS Enterprise under the command of Captain Jean-Luc Picard was not near Borg space, nor were they aware of the identity of the alien race. The first Borg encounter was initiated by Q who appeared on the Enterprise on Stardate 42761.9 in the episode "Q Who?" in the second season.

This was the third encounter with Q whereby he offered his services if Picard would allow him to become a crew member. Picard's refusal angered Q to the point of proving his point, that Picard would break down and in the end be pleading to Q to use his power to save the Enterprise and her crew from annihilation by the Borg. In his rage, Q sends the Enterprise hurling seven thousand light years from their present location to system J-25. Data's calculations revealed that even at maximum warp it would take the Enterprise 2 years, 7 months, 3 days and 18 hours to reach Starbase 85.

The sensor scanning of system J-25 revealed that the sixth planet, a Class-M, had its entire civilization annihilated and its surface looked as if it had been scoured of anything resembling colonization. The Outposts along the Neutral Zone were also attacked by the Borg. Luckily for Captain Picard, Guinan, the bartender of the Ten Forward lounge, was able to input information she knew about the Borg. She and Q also knew each other in a not so friendly manner.

The Borg would prove to be a formidable enemy to Starfleet and the United Federation of Planets, with no hope for negotiation for a peace. Their task was to turn whole civilizations into Borgs. Initial contact with the Borg allowed Captain Picard to surmise the following important points about them.

1) Initial encounter is to learn more about their enemy by sending scouts aboard the enemy ship.

2) Analyze the defensive capabilities of opponent.

3) No single leader, they operate with the collective minds of all.

4) Their tractor beam is impermeable to starship phaser/photon torpedo firing. The Borg laser can slice through the duranium hull as if it were hot butter. Shields are defenseless against the Borg particle beam. Through the collective minds, any damage to the Borg ship can be replicated even while the ship is in warp. The Borg ship can operate at peak efficiency even if twenty percent of the ship is gone.

5) Hand-to-hand combat is not recommended as the Borg possess extraordinary strength in their limbs, as well as armament.

The episodes "The Best of Both Worlds, Part 1," (the season 3 cliffhanger) and "The Best of Both Worlds, part II" (the season four premiere episode) featured the first cliff-hanger episode in the history of STAR TREK. This encounter with the Borg would leave permanent scars that would surface in the following season with yet a third encounter.

## THE BEST OF BOTH WORLDS, (Part One)

Written by Michael Piller

Directed by Cliff Bole

The story opens on Stardate 43992.6 as the Enterprise is dispatched to Jeray 4 to investigate the disappearance of all 900 inhabitants of the New Providence Colony. To assist them in their investigation, Starfleet Command sent the USS Melbourne to transport Admiral Hansen and Commander Shelby of Starfleet tactical. Starfleet Command had known the Borg were coming for over a year, but they were far from prepared. New weaponry was still on the drawing board and an alternate defense strategy had to be devised.

The Enterprise reaches the location of New Providence Colony only to find a vast crater where the settlement once stood. Admiral Hansen and Commander Shelby fear that the Borg are responsible. Commander Shelby beams down in advance of the Away Team against Riker's orders. Her analysis of the soil on Jeray 4 showed the same magnetic resonance traces as found on the Enterprise hull after the Borg attack in the J-25 system (where the Borg had removed a section of the hull for their own personal analysis).

Commander Shelby describes this resonance as a Borg footprint. Shelby, an ambitious woman, is gunning for Riker's first officer chair. Riker has been offered his own command for the third time, but wants to remain on the Enterprise. Friction develops between him and Shelby.

Stardate 43993.5. The findings on Jeray 4 confirmed that the Borg were in Federation space. Admiral Hansen returns to Starfleet Command to discuss strategy. The Enterprise as well as the entire quadrant is placed on alert status with all Federation and Allied outposts warned of the imminent danger. On board the Enterprise on standing yellow alert is ordered with OPTS to man the long range sensors for any unusual ship contacts. Analyzing battle tactics from the first Borg battle revealed:

1) A manipulation effect in the Borg subspace field—a definite pattern—at 4.8 minute intervals during the first confrontation, possibly indicating high input auxiliary generators kicking in.

2) THEORY—The entire Borg system is decentralized with redundant power sources located throughout the ship.

3) CONCLUSION—Borg technology has given each member of the Society the ability to interface collectively. It is theorized that the ship was constructed with the same philosophy.

4) PROJECTION—Even with 78% of the Borg ship inoperable, it would still function, repairing itself while in warp speed.

Admiral Hansen contacts Captain Picard to relay information about the USS Lawla, a freighter which had departed Zeta Alpha II for Zeta Minor IV, sent out a distress call which was received at Starbase 157. The call stated that they had made contact with a cube-shaped vessel. The distress call ended abruptly, and the ship had not been heard from since. At warp 9 the Enterprise would intercept the Borg ship in 1 hour 17 minutes. Commander Shelby and Lt. Cdr. LaForge plan to modulate shield mutation and return the ship's phasers as well as the hand units to higher Em base emitting frequencies to disrupt their subspace field. At 210 MARK 153, the inevitable occurs.

When the Enterprise intercepts them, they hail Picard by name, and order him to transport to their ship or be destroyed. When Picard refuses, the Borg lock a tractor beam on the Enterprise and begin cutting into her hull with a laser. Picard orders the Enterprise to change course to 151 MARK 330 to outrun the Borg after breaking free from their tractor beam.

The course takes the ship into the Pulsan Nebula, which has a composition of 82% dilithium hydroxyls, magnesium and cronium which would prove effective in screening against the Borg sensors. It would buy the Enterprise and her crew time to analyze their situation as she could not hide in the nebula for long.

At time index 514, Data starts to fluctuate phaser resonance frequencies and the Borg beam breaks contact. A two percent drop in power system wide on the Borg ship is noted when the Enterprise phaser frequency spread is on the high neural band. This proves that the Borg ship power distribution nodes are vulnerable to those frequencies.

The Borg bombard the nebula and drive the Enterprise back out. Another attack ensues, during which several Borg appear on the bridge and kidnap Picard. Once they have him, they ignore the Enterprise and head towards the heart of the Federation— Earth.

Riker is now acting commander of the Enterprise and plans to attack the Borg ship with a concentrated phaser burst through the deflector shield. An away team led by Shelby beams onto the Borg ship, where they disrupt systems and cause the ship to drop out of warp. They also discover that Picard has become a Borg before they beam back to the Enterprise.

Picard, now a Borg called Locutus, has been chosen to speak for the Borg. He demands that the Enterprise surrender. Riker, faced with what his former captain has become, gives Worf the order to fire on the Borg ship.

# THE BEST OF BOTH WORLDS (Part Two)

Written by Michael Piller

Directed by Cliff Bole

In "The Best of Both Worlds, part 2," Riker's attack on the Borg ship fails, causing extensive systems damage to the Enterprise. The Borg, having absorbed Picard into their group mind, now possess all his knowledge and experience, and resume their course to Earth. Picard's own memories and experiences have now become irrelevant as the Borg identity controls everything he thinks and says.

Admiral Hansen communicates with the Enterprise: the Federation has assembled an armada of forty of their own ships, in addition to the Klingons. They are even considering contacting the Romulans. Riker receives a field commission, and promises to join the Federation forces as soon as the Enterprise is functional again. Shelby becomes First Officer.

The reference to the Federation contacting the Romulans was originally conceived by Maurice Hurley as part of the Borg storyline. He wanted the Federation and the Romulans to unite against a common foe, but Gene Roddenberry vetoed the idea. Unfortunately the result is that the Romulans have become the one-dimensional villains that the Klingons were in the original STAR TREK series. Surely they deserve more dignity than that.

Hansen communicates again with the Enterprise: the Federation has engaged the Borg, and the battle is not going well. His transmission is cut off abruptly. When the Enterprise reaches the battle site, they find a scene of complete devastation. Riker plans to separate the saucer section of the Enterprise for a diversion. Picard knew of this plan, but Riker has altered it considerably, hoping to outwit the memories of his former mentor.

The Borg ship's magnetic field now blocks Transporter beams, so Worf and Data take a shuttle into range and use its escape transport to beam onto the Borg ship and recapture Picard/Locutus. They return to the shuttle, clear the Borg field, and beam back to the Enterprise just before the shuttle is destroyed. The two ship sections reconnect.

Picard/Locutus is still linked by subspace signal with the Borg mind. Data creates a neural link with Picard/Locutus, and eventually reaches the Borg command system. It is divided into various command sub-units, but he cannot access any of the vital areas. The Borg halt their advance on Earth and attack the Enterprise. Riker orders a last-ditch, warp-speed collision with the Borg ship. Picard's personality emerges, and repeats the word "sleep."

Crusher takes this as an expression of fatigue, but Data realizes that Picard is telling him what to do: the Borg regenerative system is of low priority, easily accessed, and Data uses it to convince the Borg that it is time for a regenerative cycle, effectively putting them all to sleep.

The Borg attack stops. A power feedback caused by this induced malfunction causes the Borg ship to self-destruct, freeing Picard from their sub-space link. The Borg machinery is removed from his body. The Enterprise docks for repair, and Shelby leaves to head the task force rebuilding the fleet. The personality of Jean-Luc Picard has re-emerged, but is he really unhurt and unscathed by the ordeal?

In a rare example of a television science fiction series dealing realistically with the probable fallout from a dramatic situation, the very next episode, titled "Family," written by Ronald D. Moore and directed by Les Landau, deals with the less spectacular side-effects of the battle with the Borg. In it, Jean-Luc Picard chooses to take a well-earned shore leave on Earth, which they had come close to in their battle with the menace from beyond our galaxy. The Enterprise, still docked for repairs, remains in orbit over Earth.

For the first time in twenty years, Picard returns to his home in France. While Picard is physically recovered from his ordeal, he still has psychological scars to contend with and has chosen to wrestle with these problems by returning home and seeing his brother.

Unresolved conflicts with his brother still remain, but Jean-Luc is prepared to confront them if necessary. His older brother, Robert, is a farmer bent on keeping the family traditions alive. Robert has always regarded Jean-Luc as arrogant and ambitious. This comes out when Jean-Luc arrives at the family estate and meets his young nephew, Rene. The boy remarks that Jean-Luc doesn't look arrogant. So even before meeting Robert we know he has a grudge against Jean-Luc. When Jean-Luc meets his brother for the first time in nearly twenty years, Robert barely says hello and acts distant and preoccupied.

Robert is Jean-Luc's older brother and appears to be in his sixties, but he still works in his vineyard. Over dinner, a small argument develops in which Robert complains that "Life is already too convenient" when the talk of getting a food synthesizer comes up. When Rene remarks that he won a ribbon for his paper on starships, Robert is clearly annoyed. The boy has already remarked to his uncle that some day he's going to be a starship captain. While Jean-Luc gets along well with Robert's young wife and son, Robert himself remains distant and critical.

The portrayal of Robert Picard is strange because it's the 24th century and yet he acts like a 20th century man railing against "progress." The thing is, life would be so different in the 24th century from what it's like today that no one in living memory would remember what it had been like in "simpler" times. The more simple times would have been hundreds of years ago.

This one aspect of Robert Picard's character does not ring true, but it can be overlooked in light of the more important issues the episode deals with. In an effort to give some perspective to Robert Picard, Jean-Luc's old friend Louis remarks at one point that Jean-Luc was always reaching for the future while Robert was reaching for the past.

Jean-Luc Picard's old friend Louis visits him; Louis is involved in a project to raise a section of the sea floor for a new sub-continent and believes that Picard would be the ideal man to direct the project. The project directors are more than eager to have Jean-Luc lead them. Picard is tempted, but uncertain. On one hand, he is dedicated to Starfleet; on the other, his experience with the Borg has left him uncertain.

Tensions mount between the Picard brothers until Jean-Luc punches Robert when they're talking in Robert's vineyard. Robert had always resented the way Jean-Luc broke every one of their father's rules and got away with it. Jean-Luc had been an athletic hero in high school as well as the school valedictorian and Robert admits that he was jealous. Robert had earlier asked what had happened to Jean-Luc out there, remarking that he understands that his brother must have been humiliated. "But then I always thought you needed a little humiliation, or a little humility."

In the vineyard they finally get to the bottom of their resentments as Jean-Luc tells Robert that he was a bully and challenges the older man to try and bully him now. Robert lashes out at his brother and a fight erupts. They roll around in the vineyard until they're covered in mud, at which point they break out laughing. Jean-Luc's laughter soon gives way to tears, for he has been unable until now to face the self-doubt raised by the Borg's use of him.

"They took everything I was. They used me to kill and to destroy and I couldn't stop them. I should have been able to stop them! I tried so hard, but I wasn't strong enough. I wasn't good enough. I should've been able to stop them!" Now that his emotions have broken through, he can begin to deal with them. Robert points out that Jean-Luc will have to live with this for a very long time, whether below the sea with Louis or in space on the Enterprise. Jean-Luc makes his decision and decides to return to command the Enterprise.

As Jean-Luc prepares to return to the Enterprise, young Rene again expresses his desire to be a starship caption. In Rene, Jean-Luc sees himself when he was a boy; a child whose eyes were always on the stars. Robert has realized this as well and has had to come to terms with the fact that his son will undoubtedly follow in his uncle's footsteps, not his father's. Even after Jean-Luc has left, Rene sits outside staring up at the stars. His mother remarks, "It's getting late." But Robert replies, "Let him dream." Both brothers have come to terms with what the future holds.

"Family" is one of the best episodes NEXT GENERATION has produced, and the fact that it has the courage to deal with human issues on a human level rather than on a galactic one makes it all the more compelling. We understand these people and how each has affected the other, for better or for worse. And each of them has to come to terms with the emotional fallout from that.

The episode also has two subplots, one involving Worf's human foster parents visiting the Enterprise and the other with Wesley watching a hologram of his father for the first time which was made at the time of the boy's birth. Try as they might, these subplots just seem like distractions from the infinitely more interesting story of Jean-Luc coming to grips with his personal demons and reconciling with his brother.

Sadly, this is one of the lowest rated episodes ST-TNG produced, and yet it is far and away one of their top ten entries. At the very least it should have been nominated for the Humanatus Award, the annual prize given to television writing which promotes strong human values. Perhaps had it dealt entirely with Picard and dispensed with the padding of the minor subplots it would have received more serious consideration.

# I, BORG

Written by Rene Echevarria

Directed by Robert Lederman

The fifth season of the series brought a return encounter with the Borg in a very different way from what might have been expected. "I Borg" takes the one-dimensional menace of the Borg and gives them a human face. After all, the Borg start out human. It's what's done to them after their born that makes them part of the cybernetic group mind.

The story opens on an uncharted region of the galaxy where the Enterprise is receiving a distress call on the second SS Beacon. Upon the Away Team beaming to the crash site, they find the wreckage of a small Borg scout ship. Out of the five aboard, four are dead but one has a chance for survival. Capt. Picard argues against this, stating that what they picked up had to be a Borg distress signal and a mothership will be on its way to answer. The Borg always retrieve their dead. Picard also points out that they shouldn't leave any signs which would give away that they had been there. Worf wants to kill the Borg youth and make it look like he died in the crash.

Dr. Crusher argues against this, even opposing Capt. Picard's statement that she should just let it die. While Dr. Crusher is, as a physician, sworn to protect all life, she doesn't explain why a Borg should evoke so much sympathy in her that she would vehemently argue to save it. Dr. Crusher is allowed to beam the Borg up to the Enterprise where Geordi blocks the homing signal so that it cannot be traced to the Enterprise should a Borg ship arrive in the area. The Borg is beamed to a holding cell even though Dr. Crusher argues to take it to sickbay, but Picard remains adamant about this.

Cut off from the group mind, Geordi and others are able to actually communicate with the Borg, but Picard refuses to consider that it could have a personality and at first refuses to even go down and look at it. He is clearly haunted by the memories of what the Borg did to him. Ultimately this gives Picard an idea. What if they could use this Borg to sabotage the collective minds? This could be accomplished by incorporating a thought, or an idea, which would create a paradox in the group mind. The use of the paradox would cause complete systems failure throughout the entire Borg collective, annihilating their entire race.

Interestingly, throughout this episode, Captain Picard does not once make a Captain's Log report to Starfleet Command apprising them of their situation. Possibly it was to cover any decisions he might make out of his anger towards the Borg after his last encounter and abduction.

Geordi, LaForge and Dr. Crusher continue to study the Borg, whose only identity was "third of five." But after their introductions, the Borg asked if he too had a name. A name befitting to Geordi and Beverly was "Hugh," and after only a few introductions, the Borg was referring to himself in the singular form, not the collective. But Captain Picard absolutely cannot accept Geordi and Beverly treating this Borg as a person, even to the point of giving him a name. That was until Guinan paid Hugh a visit where she found human characteristics surfacing and the Borg referring to himself in the singular sense.

After much soul-searching, Captain Picard agrees to meet Hugh in his office. Hugh recognizes Picard as Locutus, and Picard uses the situation to his advantage to see if Hugh still has any loyalties to the Borg collective, but Hugh did not. Hugh states in a very upset manner that Geordi did not wish to be assimilated. But when Picard insists that he would have no choice were the Borg to capture him, Hugh says that Geordi is a friend. Yes, a friend. At this point even the viewers experience the pain that the young Borg is feeling. We began to like this enemy, or at least this individual.

Long range sensors pick up the Borg ship entering the star system. Hugh is given a choice by Picard to either return to the crash site or be given asylum and remain with them on the Enterprise. To be given a choice is hard for Hugh to comprehend as he has never been given one before. He chooses to return to the crash site as it would be too dangerous for him to stay, yet he did not want to keep his memories of being on the Enterprise and the friends he had made. It would be dangerous were the Borg collective to discover what had happened.

The Enterprise hides in the corona of the star in order to remain undetected by the arriving Borg ship. Geordi accompanies Hugh to the surface. Not long after they beam down the Borg arrive and pick up Hugh. The Borg ignore Geordi just as they ordinarily do when someone not a part of the collective is nearby.

Just before materialization is complete, Hugh turns to look at Geordi as he had retained his singular thought, even after being assimilated back into the collective. It is believed that the concept of individuality could also prove destructive to the Borg, but in a completely different way. After all, how would one react to the concept of free will when they had never known of the existence of the concept before?

Perhaps at the next encounter with the Borg, the idea of a singular being would be widespread throughout the collective and yes, perhaps Hugh would not be destroyed. Instead he might prove to be the space seed for a new generation of the Borg, with each one as a singular being.

When the Borg were introduced in year two, they were the ultimate villains. Now they are starting to emerge as a race capable of producing beings with a personality. "I,Borg" demonstrates the possibilities in future stories dealing with the Borg as their existence has enriched the entire tapestry and creative texture of the series.

# THE NEXT GENERATION
# WE NEVER SAW

*When STAR TREK—THE NEXT GENERATION was first gearing up in 1987, many story ideas were submitted before the show finally took shape. The following unused story lines demonstrate the early approaches taken to stories featuring these new characters, as well as directions never followed.*

# UNFILMED EPISODES

$\mathbb{T}$he following stories were developed for production on ST-TNG but for various reasons never aired. This is generally because a consensus can never be arrived at on how to make the story work or just because other scripts were deemed better. Most television series have scripts which are written but never aired.

One of the most famous unfilmed episodic TV scripts was from M*A*S*H and involved Hawkeye Pierce being forced to use a gun to shoot a Korean soldier in order to save one of his friends. A workable ending was never developed in which Hawkeye could convincingly justify what he had to do. Many attempts were made but ultimately the script was abandoned. That's just one example of the kinds of decisions which cause a script to be shelved.

It's up to you to decide whether any of these stories deserves to be resurrected now that THE NEXT GENERATION is in its sixth season.

## "THE BONDING"

written by Lee Maddux (10-9-87)

Synopsis: Captain Jean-Luc Picard's is ordered to monitor a territorial dispute between two neighboring Federation worlds. His job: to come up with a treaty the two worlds can agree on. At the computer station on the bridge he, Riker, Worf and Data are intent on analyzing star maps of the area of space under dispute, when Worf becomes strangely agitated and distracted. Picard tells Worf to pay attention to his work — a gentle reprimand — and Data meets Worf's eyes with a curious gaze.

In various scenes, ordinary day-use of the computer is portrayed, showing crew members activating it for, among many things, food preparation, uniform mending, and turbolift transportation.

Suddenly, the Enterprise is called away from its mission to look into current civil disturbances on the planet Omega Croton IV. Refugees of the disturbances are in need of medical assistance, and the Enterprise must transport them to a medical base. The two disputing planets understand and accept that the Enterprise must leave.

En route to Omega Croton IV, Data tells what he knows of the inhabitants they will be transporting. They are, he says, a humanoid race of people who have super-telekinetic powers and use those powers to supply a species known as Subjects with everything they wish for. As soon as they are in orbit, they begin to beam aboard refugees. From the crowd, an older woman with a baby slips away and enters an empty room. She puts the child in an air-duct, then collapses to the deck. It is as if the life just leaves her body. The baby, a boy, makes a gurgling noise and the computer responds by blowing warm air over him and creating a "web-like diaper" to drape him with.

Later, with the 'refugee' mission completed, the Enterprise returns to the two worlds in need of a treaty. This time, it is Geordi who notices that Worf isn't acting normal. Meanwhile, the baby is still in the air duct. A clear pack of baby formula appears out of the air and floats to the baby. The baby begins to suckle from it. The sound of a burp alerts an engineer who, curious, enters the room and discovers the body of the woman.

The body is taken to sickbay where Dr. Crusher discovers that the woman is a Croton, not a Subject as was thought because her skin color is blue (the color of the Subject's skin.) Crusher says the woman altered her skin color to pass as a Subject, and that she died by willing herself to die. The captain demands a more thorough autopsy. In another scene, Deanna Troi and Data discuss Worf's recent peculiar behavior and conclude that it must be too personal for him to discuss. Data decides to keep a close watch on him and inform Troi of any change.

On the bridge, Picard contacts Starfleet with news of the woman's death. He informs them an autopsy is being done. Worf announces that his scanners are picking up an ion storm. The captain orders up full shielding. It's a rough ride as the scene cuts to the child, still in the air duct, crying from fear.

Back on the bridge, Picard is annoyed when the Enterprise goes around the storm instead of through it as he ordered. He thinks it is Geordi who changed the course, but Geordi denies having anything to do with it. Apparently, the computer took control of the ship in that instant, and no one knows why. Picard activates the computer and asks it why it took control of the ship. The computer answers by saying that its "child" was in danger by the storm, so it took control to avoid the storm. The scene cuts to show the air duct again. In it, the child, now an older version of himself, is quietly sleeping.

Troi and Data investigate the systems and find out that the computer has been transporting supplies to the 'child'. The computer finally decides to tell them the location of the boy. Picard leaves the bridge, after giving Riker orders to keep on course, then heads for sickbay. The scene cuts to show Tasha Yar taking the child from the air duct and handing it over to medical personnel. The child now appears to be about eighteen months old.

In sickbay, Crusher tells Picard that through the help of a special new machine, the thoughts of the person's last hours alive can be viewed visually. Back on the bridge, Worf sees that Data is researching "Abnormal Behavior In Klingons" and is quite distraught. Data reacts guiltily. The scene cuts to sickbay again, where Picard and Crusher are viewing the deceased's final hours of life. She walks into a Croton temple where someone hands her the baby.

As soon as she leaves the building, the temple explodes. She covers the baby with her tunic, and runs away. Further details reveal that the boy is Croton's ruler. Before they can continue, pediatrics reports that something is peculiar with the boy. Picard and Riker arrive to find themselves face to face with a very intelligent child who looks to be about ten years old. He tells them in a strange monotone that his name is Pattrue, that he has computerized intelligence, and that he wishes asylum on board the Enterprise until the problems on his world, Croton Omega, are solved. Picard considers this.

Picard returns to the bridge and asks Data and Riker for advice on what to do with the boy. Geordi informs them that something has invaded the ship's computer system and is sucking out incredible amounts of information chunks. Picard decides that someone on board is responsible and orders Tasha and Riker to investigate. Their trail ends in a corridor where they find Pattrue floating before a computer terminal absorbing information from it.

Riker orders the computer to stop. It refuses. It explains that the child must have the information it is taking in order to complete his mission. Apparently, the Crotons have stagnated, and need new information to

**97**

keep life interesting. This is the reason for the Subjects' revolt. Data discovers that the information is not being taken and erased, simply 'shared' with the boy.

Picard worries that the Prime Directive may be in question here, and contacts Starfleet command. They answer immediately, saying they have heard from the Crotons and the Subjects, who say they will cease all hostility if Pattrue is returned. Picard agrees to return him as soon as he's completed the survey for the two planets having territorial disputes.

While the Enterprise finishes its mission, Wesley and Pattrue become acquainted. Wesley gives Pattrue a tour of the Enterprise and introduces him to emotions, which the boy has never experienced. Feelings are a mystery to Pattrue. Also, Data has finally discovered what is bothering Worf. The 20 year anniversary for his initiation rites into warriorship is coming up. It involves a complex, ritualistic ceremony. Worf is excused from the bridge. Picard gives permission for Geordi, Tasha and Data to surprise Worf with a ritual ceremony.

Wesley and Pattrue witness a couple laughing and embracing. But Pattrue still does not understand emotion. Data, Geordi and Tasha acquire "pain sticks" for Worf's surprise ritual. The ritual involves an attack on Worf by his friends. Data comments that attacking Worf (even for his own good) is akin to standing in front of a launched photon torpedo.

A while later, Wesley and Pattrue are walking by Worf's quarters when they hear screaming inside. They run in to find Worf being attacked and beaten down by Data, Tasha and Geordi. Pattrue moves to assist Worf but Wesley holds him back explaining that Worf is "celebrating" by being humiliated in this way. As Worf gives in, he tearfully thanks Data, Tasha and Geordi for the finest humiliation he's ever experienced.

Pattrue is amazed. He thinks what Worf's friends have done for him is truly inspirational. On his homeworld, nothing can compare. True friendship, sentiment, compassion, selflessness such as this, is not logical or allowed. Pattrue enters the bridge the inform Picard that now he does not wish to return to his home because he cannot tolerate living on a world that scorns expression of emotion.

Picard discusses the situation with Doctor Crusher and Wesley. Pattrue must return to his homeworld, or the civil unrest will continue. Picard thinks Wesley may be the only one who can convince Pattrue of the importance of this. Wesley visits Pattrue in sickbay and tries to get his friend to change his mind. Pattrue refuses, and states that his people must work out their problems on their own.

Picard calls the boys to the bridge. Pattrue witnesses, on the viewscreen, a battle being fought near the Royal Palace. With his new ability to feel, Pattrue is very moved by the violence. He is the only one who can stop it, so he agrees to return. But will the Crotons accept a ruler who has emotions? Since the law of the planet is based on a caste system, all beings are considered equal. Therefore, Pattrue concludes, the law against emotion is outdated and void. He hopes to lead his people to true brotherhood, where emotions will be viewed as assets.

In the Transporter room, Pattrue says good-bye to Wesley. As he beams away, the Enterprise computer gives its own farewell. "Go in peace."


Commentary: This episode is too complex, with too many subplots that are treated as less important than they should be. It cannot be adequately portrayed in an hour-long teleplay. For example, the subplot about Worf has nothing to do with the rest of the story, except that through Worf, Pattrue finally learns and understands the value of emotion. Also, the map survey and treaty for the two Federation planets having a territorial dispute is just an excuse to show that the Enterprise keeps herself and her crew busy.

It is a time-waster, especially since it seems no one, including the writer, seems to care much about these planets and their dispute. The idea of the telekinetic Crotons and Subjects is never fleshed out. The society is complex enough to warrant its own hour-long episode to explain its intricacies.

Also, the computer's human-like response to the child is never fully investigated or examined by the crew. That in itself is an interesting but unlikely story, which could be developed in its own episode. This treatment is overly dramatic, unconvincing, and confusing. The idea that Worf needs to be humiliated and hurt by friends to alleviate his mental anguish pertaining to a 20 year anniversary of instilling warrior rites seems utterly ridiculous. And yet, this subplot, slightly altered, is used in a later episode, "The Icarus Factor." In "The Icarus Factor," Data, Geordi and Wesley are the ones who assist in the ceremony. Afterwards, Worf thanks them for helping him 'celebrate'. According to credits, writer Lee Maddux is given no credit for assisting in the story or script, though the subplot does seem to be lifted right out of this outline of "The Bonding."

Also, the idea of a rapidly aging child is used in the episode "The Child" in second season. ("The Child" was also a rewrite of an episode proposed for a Star Trek series in the 70's.) Furthermore, the plot about Pattrue trying to understand emotions parallels Data's own quest, yet that 'shared concern' is ignored in this treatment.

# "BLOOD AND FIRE"

written by David Gerrold

Synopsis: The Enterprise Away Team, consisting of Tasha, Riker, Geordi, Freeman, Hodel and Eakins is about to beam over to the research ship Copernicus. Copernicus sent out a distress signal and is now adrift and silent.

On the bridge, they set up to monitor the progress of the Away Team. Worf picks up a repulsor field in the other ship's cargo bay. The repulsor field is an isolation field.

The Away Team appears in a dark corridor. A subliminal flash of pink/gold light floats above them. All is silent. The ship appears dead. They see the light again, and Geordi refers to it as a "wavicle." The light surrounds him and tickles him. No one can explain the phenomenon. On the ship, Picard and Data begin to analyze the light. As the Away Team progresses through the ship, they encounter sealed, locked doors. They must use manual access to get to the bridge. Along the way, Data calls from the ship to say they are picking up weak life readings.

On the bridge of the Copernicus they encounter a dead, mummified body. They joke about 'space vampires' while Geordi downloads the log. Data calls to say the weak life reading is heading their way. The bridge door opens and Ahrens enters, a sick, haggard-looking man. He cries out that they are too late, everyone is dead.

Freeman injects the man with a hypo. Ahrens screams and begs them to kill him. Then he collapses, blood soaking the clothing at his chest. Pink/gold wavicles come out of him and enter the Away Team. Data tells them that the weak life readings are still approaching. Riker believes the wavicles have infected them with whatever has killed the Copernicus' crew. They cannot beam back to the ship. Picard orders them to the cargo bay where the repulsor field is. He hopes the remaining crew have isolated themselves there, and have some answers.

On the Enterprise, Data and Dr. Crusher inform Picard that the wavicles infecting the Away Team seem to be plasmasites, or 'bloodworms'. There is no cure, and no one is known to have survived. The only other place this disease was found was on Regula, which has been quarantined for over 100 years. It is against regulations to try to rescue anyone with 'bloodworms'.

On the Copernicus, Hodel and Eakins work on activating the dead computer. They discuss how long Eakins and Freeman have 'been together' (two years) and mention their Academy days together. This is a subtle way to establish Freeman and Eakins as lovers. They get the computer working and start downloading to the Enterprise.

Hodel reaches into a panel and screams. Red worms start coming out. Something has bit his hand and the worms are on his hand. He can't get them off and starts screaming as they move over his body. Eakins phasers a pile of worms on the floor and they turn into wavicles. Eakins moves away from the suffering Hodel who is now covered with the worms.

He fires his phaser at him and Hodel disintegrates, releasing more gold/pink wavicles. Riker and Tasha appear behind Eakins, and all three decide to run for it. Freeman appears, and asks, with concern, if Eakins is all right. Eakins responds by trying to justify what he did. Picard calls to confirm that what they are seeing are, indeed, Regulan blood worms.

The Away Team knows that this means they have no hope of rescue. But Picard devises a way to transport them to the repulsor field in the cargo bay. They materialize in an area with about fifteen survivors. Freeman, the med-tech, sees to their injuries. They are informed that the Copernicus mission was authorized to break quarantine and discern whether or not they had the technology to neutralize plasmasites. Geordi learns that the repulsor field will only hold for a short time, and that it is surrounded by worms.

On the Enterprise, Dr. Crusher has come up with a plan to remove all blood from infected persons, and then give them new blood. But the procedure cannot take more than ten minutes, or the patient will die. A particular Starfleet regulation states the 'critically important' personnel can be rescued from extremely hostile situations. Riker wants the sick people taken first, however.

Dr. Crusher volunteers to beam over into the repulsor field. Picard tries to talk her out of it, saying that if anything happened to her, Wes would be orphaned. But her oath as a physician urges her to help the sick and dying. Worf beams her over and when Picard asks for his opinion on the matter, he says, "You're asking me as a Klingon? Beat her. As a professional... she was right."

On the bridge, Picard learns that the families on board don't want to take the risk of beaming aboard contaminated survivors. Picard says the ship is not run by democracy. "We're not throwing away half the human race because the other half is scared."

Beverly has an auxiliary sickbay set up, and two people are beamed over. She also learns that Regulan bloodworms come from a doomsday device created by one side during a war. Geordi tells them they have forty minutes before the repulsor field collapses.

On the bridge, Picard allows Wesley to stay to monitor his mother. Wesley asks why Starfleet sends families to space when it is so dangerous. Picard's answer: "Because our ancestors took their children with them when they crossed the oceans in ships and the continents in covered wagons. Because —you are our children and we cannot leave you behind."

On the Copernicus, Eakins sits by Freeman and Freeman tells him he always worries about Eakins because Eakins is in security which is the most dangerous field.

Meanwhile, Data and Dr. Crusher, on communicators from the two ships, discuss the fact that the wavicles are what spread the disease, and therefore they cannot contain the infestation. They also discover they don't have enough blood for complete transfusions for all afflicted, and those on the Enterprise must donate blood.

Yarell and Blodgett, the two men beamed from Copernicus to the special sickbay and who now appear cured, tell Picard that an undeclared state of war exists between the Federation and Ferengi Alliance. They authorized the mission because they were afraid the Ferengi would use bloodworms as a weapon, and they needed to study the bloodworms to find a cure or to 'contain' the infestation. They had made good progress in their studies, but the information is not on the computer because they couldn't risk the Ferengi getting the information. Picard has security confine the men to quarters.

Geordi and Tasha are beamed aboard now that their transfusions have been completed. Riker and Freeman are next. Eakins will be the last one out.

On the Copernicus, Freeman and Eakins argue about leaving one or the other behind. Freeman won't leave first, and injects Riker and Eakins with an enzyme suppressant. As Eakins loses consciousness, he hands Freeman a phaser and says, "Just in case." Riker and Eakins are beamed away.

The repulsor field weakens. It collapses and Freeman tells the Transporter room he can hear worms approaching. The Transporter locks onto Freeman, but scanners indicate he still has plasmasites in him. Eakins calls out to him over the communicator, Freeman says he's sorry and screams. A sound of phaser fire is heard, then static.

Dr. Crusher tells Picard that the Copernicus can't simply be destroyed, because it will release wavicles which will eventually find a world with blood-filled beings and the horror will begin again. Also, Dr. Crusher believes the wavicles are trying to metamorphosize into another form, and that is why they're so aggressive. If she can alter what makes them hungry, they will stop vampirizing people.

Of course, to test her 'cure' she would need a human volunteer. At the same time, Picard learns that the Copernicus is not drifting aimlessly, but is heading directly for Ferengi space. He has Yarell brought to the bridge and Yarell confesses he is sending bloodworms to the Ferengi to 'protect' the Federation. Picard wants to stop the ship, but Yarell holds a repulsor jar of plasmasites which he says he will release if they and the Copernicus is not allowed to continue on to Ferengi space to be released.

Eakins steps on the bridge with a phaser and threatens Yarell, saying he is responsible for killing everyone on Copernicus including Freeman. Weeping, he finally hands his phaser to Riker. Then Yarell screams and everyone sees Blodgett with the repulsor vial. He swallows it, then requests to be beamed to Copernicus. He says he will be the human volunteer for Dr. Crusher's 'cure'. He is beamed over and wavicles surround him. Whatever cure Dr. Crusher came up with to alter the plasmasites makes Blodgett glow and then disappear and become light.

On the Enterprise, Wesley watches and compares the lights to a the legend of a 'sparkle dancer'. The light moves like "a colony of dancing butterflies of light and energy." The Federation is safe now that they know how to transform the wavicles into this form of energy.

Commentary: This is an interesting episode full of dark possibilities as far as directing it goes. It is filled with horrific images. If done right, it could be as scary as ALIEN. David Gerrold has said himself that when he wrote the script from this story, it was loved by all.

Then the script was suddenly canceled. David was told by a person in a position at Paramount who knew the internal things that were going on that Gene Roddenberry's lawyer thought the script was terrible and on the strength of that one opinion it was shelved. David wrote this script to address very serious issues such as what you do with people who are contaminated, how you deal with the fear that keeps you from helping them, etc., because this very thing is going on in relation to AIDS in this world.

He also wrote in a few subtle scenes showing two characters who could be gay (or just friends, if you didn't read between the lines) in order to address the fact that no gay characters have ever been shown in the Star Trek universe, and many fans have made it known that they'd like the subject addressed. Whatever caused the script to be shelved, it is obvious that a good story with very interesting character interplay has been wasted. The 'loss' of this story can only hurt THE NEXT GENERATION.

So far, no gay characters have been seen on the Enterprise. There have been episodes that border on dealing with the theme. "The Host" (fourth season) deals with a symbiotic parasite that is the real intelligence that inhabits mindless, zombie-like humanoid bodies to survive. In "The Host," Dr. Crusher falls in love with one of these aliens. His host body is destroyed, and he must be transferred to a new body.

In the end, his new body is female. It makes no difference to him, but to Beverly Crusher it is just too much to handle. Even though she really loved this person, she was also apparently very attached to his 'male' body. She cannot deal with her love in the form of a female. For many people, this episode was frustrating, a cop out. For others, like myself, I felt that it dealt realistically with the limitations humans can still have, even in the twenty-fourth century, concerning how far their 'human' cultural conditioning goes.

Where there are human beings, there will always be prejudice, and always those who cannot accept into their lives things that are truly abnormal to them. Who can blame them? Most people I know abhor disruption of their life routines, and fight change. And people who are involved in same sex relationships don't do it to be strange or eccentric, they do so because it is `normal' for them.

For Beverly Crusher, this is not 'normal'. This is what that episode addressed. Another episode which aired in fifth season, "Outcast," shows us a society of people who are all one sex. (They are, strangely, all played by androgynous-looking women. They all wear the same clothes, have the same haircuts, etc. It is as if to be only one sex you all have to look like clones of one another. Gimme a break.) When one of the people of this society feels what are defined to be "female" tendencies, and falls in love with Riker, this is looked on by 'her' fellow people as a perversion.

They eventually take 'her' to be healed/repaired (I don't remember the exact term) so that these tendencies 'she' has will go away. Riker fights in her world's court of law for her rights but loses. This episode appears to be a highly obvious metaphor for the gay rights issue. And yet, not once does Riker ever compare her dilemma to Earth's past when gays were 'outcast' so to speak.

Not once is the term 'homosexual' used. It is as if ST-TNG is an alternate universe where nobody is gay, but if you were, it would be 'all right'. So, to get back to "Blood and Fire," it would appear that TNG still has a long way to go in addressing this very issue. I can't believe that Gerrold's story was rejected for the simple reason that two of the characters in it are gay. That could easily have been written out.

A second treatment of "Blood and Fire" does exist, written by David Gerrold and rewritten by Herb Wright. (I suspect this rewritten version is by Herb Wright alone, using Gerrold's story.) The changes are minimal. Gone is the AIDS allegory. Gone are the characters Eakins and Freeman. Instead of bloodworms killing humans and looking for more, they have a kind of mass intelligence that manipulates the dead human body so that is lurches and stumbles like a George Romero zombie.

The zombies attack other 'live' humans in order to spread the disease. Also, when a zombie is phasered into oblivion, the wavicles from the first draft appear and can contaminate anyone nearby. Dr. Crusher finds an antidote by creating an anti-bloodworm which eats the bloodworms, then has a drug which will kill the anti-bloodworm.

This draft has some very horrific deaths, and is as scary as the first draft. Also, the bad guy is not Yarell, but an alien who is an enemy of the Federation. On Copernicus, just before the Away Team are beamed away and as the repulsor field fails, the alien threatens them with a phaser. A very irritated Worf picks him up and throws him to the zombies who tear him apart. Then the Away Team, and survivors who were frozen to slow the bloodworm infestation in them, are beamed to safety, the cure is in hand, and the Copernicus explodes. (The repulsor field sucked energy from the ship causing the antimatter to ignite, or whatever.) The Enterprise warps away to avoid being caught in the very powerful antimatter explosion. The end.

All in all, had this version or the first draft been made, it would have been an episode that would long haunt the viewer. The plot is dark, haunting, terrifying. It would have depicted with graphic pessimism the often too true horror of the unknown.

## "CHILDREN OF THE LIGHT"

Story by Michael Okuda

Synopsis: While scanning the planets in a star system they are studying in advance of its sun going nova, Wesley picks up a radio signal from the fifth planet. Its nature indicates the presence of life even though the star system is supposed to be lifeless. Riker orders the Enterprise to proceed to the fifth planet to investigate.

Upon arriving at the planet, they discover that the source of the signal is an automated distress beacon. The planet is indeed dead, but ruins there indicate that it once supported a vast civilization, including the remains of a space port. Data states that indications are that the planet was abandoned years before the star, Beta Delphi, began to flare up. But Riker is curious about the people who lived there. If they left the planet, where did they go? Or if they didn't leave, could they be in hiding?

Due to the buildup in the star, the Enterprise has only limited time to investigate the planet before it is consumed by the supernova. Worf has traced the distress beacon to a source below the surface of the planet. An Away Team consisting of Riker, Troi, Geordi and Tasha beam down to one of the vast network of tunnels below the planet's surface.

They encounter the source of the beacon as well as people who seemed to be expecting them. The Away Team is brought before the Council where one of them, Chadrona, explains that they are the Children of the Light. When Riker explains that they must evacuate immediately, Chadrona has no idea what he's talking about and insists that they have nothing to worry about.

The Away Team is briefly locked in a room but soon escape and encounter more people who are not a part of the Children of the Light. One of the guards they met earlier takes one of these people prisoner. The prisoner is brought before the Council and put on trial for activating the distress beacon and luring the "aliens" to their world. The prisoner, Doran, states that the alien can save some of their people, but the Council refuses to listen and condemns Doran for not having faith in the teachings of the Life-giver. Doran condemns the Council for worshipping death instead of life just before he's executed.

The Away Team slips away and encounters Lyrel and Kyran, two leaders of the opposition. Doran was Kyran's father. They reveal that the Council has known of the impending supernova for centuries and consider its coming a rite of passage even though they know that it will destroy everyone on the planet.

Troi explains that the Children of the Light worship the sun, and when Beta Delphi explodes, it will mean the end of their "god." The Council believes that at the instant of supernova, the people will join with the "life-giver" (as they refer to the star). Some of the people on the planet had attempted to build spacecraft to escape, but the Council wouldn't allow it. Just then guards arrive and capture the Away Team and the others they were talking with. They are put on trial and given a death sentence. Chadrona says that she envies the fact that they will unite with the Life-giver before them.

Riker breaks from his guards, grabs a tri-corder and presses a button which transmits all the information the mission gathered. Picard recognizes this as a distress signal and beams the Away Team back aboard, along with Lyrel and Kyran.

On the Enterprise, Lyrel pleads with Picard to rescue her people. Picard feels that this could violate the Prime Directive. Riker points out that if they don't act, the people will definitely die. Troi argues that this would be a violation of the Prime Directive, stating that it was established to prevent interference with alien cultures whose values are so different from our own that we have a hard time understanding or sympathizing with them. That certainly sounds like a description of the Children of the Light.

Using the holodeck, Data has the information from the tri-corder used to recreate the council chamber. Then they beam the council there to get them out of the way temporarily so that the Away Team can return to the planet.

Data uses the underground communication network to offer anyone the chance who wants to escape the destruction. Only a few people accept the opportunity, which bothers Riker. He wants to rescue as many as possible, but Troi points out that most of the people seem to be ready to accept the Rite of Passage. Picard chooses to beam up those who volunteered as the star is approaching a critical stage. The Away Team and those who wish to be rescued are returned to the Enterprise. The Council is returned to their real chamber, but not before Chaldrona and Riker have one final face to face meeting. Chaldrona hopes that Riker will one day find the peace that she is looking forward to experiencing. Riker beams up.

The Enterprise escapes at warp speed while observing the effects of the super nova. Wesley states that at the moment that the planet was destroyed, there was an energy surge recorded. Lyrel states that perhaps the Children of the Light did become one with the Life Giver after all. Worf dismisses this as superstition, but Picard isn't so sure.

Commentary: It's unknown why this story was never produced. It's actually much better than many which were. It deserves to be resurrected. Michael Okuda, the writer, remains a member of the technical crew on ST-TNG.

## "THE CRYSTAL SKULL"

written by Patrick Barry

Synopsis: An archaeologist, Dr. Annette Boudreau, studying the desert world Bolaxnu 7, has found the lost city Izul. The Faran Empire mysteriously fell 8000 years ago. Bolaxnu is located midway between Federation and Ferengi territories.

The Enterprise delivers supplies to the archeological team, and Riker, Data, Worf, Wesley, Dr. Crusher and a med-tech beam down. Beautiful ruins surround them. Dr. Boudreau appears with two of her team, and Riker is instantly taken with her handsome looks. She tells them one of her team, a man named Roark, has been injured. Beverly is taken to an underground facility where the man is. Riker quizzes Boudreau about Izul, and she tells him her findings are unconfirmed. The discussion is interrupted when someone else demands her attention.

Riker walks through the ruins, encountering the exploring Data and Worf. Data says the discovery is major. It could give insight into the Ferengi, whose home world is supposedly a stranded colony of the Faran Empire. Riker tells Data that the findings may be premature. He leaves to check on Dr. Crusher and finds her in a room holding a crystal skull. She seems to be in a trance state. When he speaks to her she becomes agitated and yells at him to leave. Curious, Riker reaches out and touches the skull. He begins to smile as he takes it from her.

Later, Boudreau demands that Riker return the missing skull. He says he will, but not yet. Then he kisses her.

On the Enterprise, Geordi detects a Ferengi vessel approaching. Troi senses obsession, but has no context for the feeling. Picard calls Riker on the planet below and tells him to be alert. The Away Team should be ready to beam up on short notice.

On the planet, Boudreau thinks the Ferengi have come for revenge. They want the artifacts in the ruins, namely, the skull. Riker tells her everything will be all right, and hides the skull in a leather bag. Data informs them of a bit of Faran history. According to myth, Faran's emperor, Doshin, was actually many rulers who took on that name. Each ruler possessed the skull which was said to have special powers. The myth of skull is to the Ferengi what the Holy Grail would be to humans.

Picard calls and tells Riker that the sensors are having trouble keeping the Away Team in sight since they are underground. Since the Ferengi are near, he wants to beam them up now. The archeological team have no communicators, so Riker gives his to the injured man. Worf gives his to Boudreau. The rest of the people without communicators must go to the surface where the transporter can pick them up easier. Wes, Dr. Crusher, the med-tech, Boudreau and the sick man are beamed up. The ones left behind head for the surface.

On the bridge, Picard receives a message from Zaeb, the Ferengi captain. Zaeb accuses Picard of being on a spy mission. He picked up a message from a person named Boudreau bragging about discovering a crystal skull. The Ferengi claim ownership of the planet and demand all Federation people vacate it at once. Picard disagrees, and says the planet was first discovered by the Federation, so it belongs to the Federation. Sensors indicate a Ferengi landing party has beamed down. Picard warns Zaeb that if the Ferengi harm anyone on the surface, the Enterprise will respond harshly.

On the planet, Riker and group encounter the landing party. Riker smiles as the Ferengi draw their weapons. (There is a reference here to "blue-skinned oriental looking Kakiri Warriors" with weapons.) Luug, commander of the landing party, demands Riker turn over all weapons. They are now prisoners of the Alliance. Riker laughs, and tells them they will never get the skull if anyone is harmed, because he has it rigged to be destroyed if anything happens.

Riker demands that they negotiate, and that Picard be present. Luug can do nothing but agree, since he wants the skull intact. Everyone but Worf and Riker and the Ferengi are beamed up to safety. Picard and Dr. Boudreau are instructed to beam down in an hour. Riker discusses possible terms with Luug, stating that he and Picard are interested in unofficial trading in which the crystal skull would be part of the trade. Then, he and Luug are drawn into a conversation about Ferengi philosophy.

On the Enterprise, Picard is confused and wants to beam down immediately.

On the planet, Worf is disturbed because he thinks Riker is lying about the skull, and lying, to a Klingon, is a dishonor. Riker is unconcerned, assuring Worf he has a plan. He sends Worf away to check on some tunnels for possible emergency escape routes should anything go wrong.

An Away Team led this time by Picard beams down underground. With him are Troi, Tasha, security agents and Boudreau. They call out for Riker and Worf but get no answer. Scene cuts to Riker in Boudreau's chamber holding the skull in his hands, his features set in a trance. Then he hears Picard calling and hides the skull. Riker goes to meet him and tells Picard that negotiations must include only himself, Picard, Boudreau, Data and the Ferengi. Everyone else must beam back to the ship. He sidesteps all their questions with a knowing smile.

On the ship, Roark, the injured man, comes to and mumbles about a crystal skull and a woman. Beverly doesn't understand his ravings. Back on the planet, Riker tells Troi he wants to talk to her about feelings never expressed but is distracted when Picard says it's time to go to the surface. He, Riker, Data and Boudreau leave the others behind. On the way through the tunnels, Riker knocks out Data (turns him off?) and Boudreau attacks Picard.

They take their phasers and communicators. Boudreau points out that now she and Riker can share the skull, then Riker knocks her out. He phasers the walls to induce a cave in so no one can follow, then leaves the area alone, goes back to Boudreau's chamber and retrieves the skull. He encounters Worf as he's leaving and tells him that the Ferengi Kakiri warriors betrayed them and killed Picard, Data, and Boudreau. Riker and Worf beam up.

On the ship, Riker assumes command and contacts Zaeb to accuse him of the murders of their shipmates. Zaeb has no idea what he's talking about, but Riker tells him if they don't surrender in ten minutes, their ship will be destroyed. The Enterprise goes to red alert.

On the planet, Data 'comes to' (??), and revives Picard and Boudreau. Boudreau tells them the truth of the skull, explaining that it gives great pleasure, then controls you. You become its tool. To escape the cave in, Boudreau finds a laser shovel and they begin to dig their way out.

On the ship, Troi tries to tell Riker that she senses Zaeb is not responsible. Troi is also very distraught over learning Picard is dead. Riker tries to embrace her but she pushes away and leaves the bridge. In sickbay, Roark is now making more sense. He explains to Dr. Crusher that Boudreau pushed him into a pit because of the skull, and that is how he was injured. They discuss events, and in Roark's opinion, Riker is being influenced by the skull.

Dr. Crusher meets with Troi and Wes and tells them their theory. She suggests Troi try to 'feel' if Picard is still alive on the planet. She asks Wes if he can manage to communicate with the planet without the bridge detecting it. Wes sets off to make the attempt. Troi goes to the bridge to keep an eye on Riker. Riker is going a bit nuts, telling Zaeb that he plans to destroy Izul with the Enterprise photon torpedoes, and that his people must beam up. He appears fatigued.

Later, Riker sits in Picard's quarters with the skull in his hand. Worf calls to say he's awaiting the order to fire on the city. Riker returns to the bridge rejuvenated. Troi questions his orders. Riker simply smiles and turns to Worf to give the order. Troi touches him and pleads with him to reverse his decision. She suggests they leave the bridge together for 'time alone' before he gives the order.

He is taken by her (hormones flaming) and agrees. Just as they arrive at the captain's quarters, Geordi calls saying an unauthorized transmission has been sent to the planet. Infuriated, Riker runs back to the bridge shouting about spies. Again, just as he is about to order destruction of the city, he is interrupted by Troi, and the Ferengi commander calls. Zaeb demands they leave or attack.

Dr. Crusher and Wesley beam up the Away Team and Picard calls to the bridge to resume command. Riker is shocked to hear Picard's voice. He accuses the Ferengi of cloning their dead shipmates, and that the clones must be destroyed. He rushes to the captain's quarters, gets the skull and brings it back to the bridge. He convinces Worf that no one else is to be trusted, and he and the Klingon leave for the battle bridge. Geordi learns that the turbo is cut off so no one else can get to the battle bridge. Picard thinks Riker is going to implement a saucer separation. He cannot beam in because there is a force field erected around the battle bridge.

On the battle bridge, Riker orders Worf to implement saucer separation, then fire on the city and on the Ferengi. Worf is unsure, but Riker smiles at him and reassures him that this day will go down in history; they will be heroes and as a result be assigned their own commands.

Picard appears on the main screen and tells Riker to think for himself, fight the skull's influence. Riker laughs, but keeps glancing at the bag where the skull is hidden. He gives Worf the order again to fire on the city, but Worf has now noticed the bag and wants to know what's inside it. Riker goes to the controls to launch the torpedoes himself, but Worf pulls him away. Riker grabs for the skull but Worf knocks it from his hands. A fight ensues. Riker picks up a phaser which he fires, but Worf dodges. The phaser fire hits the skull. Riker collapses.

Back on the bridge, Picard has resumed command. Worf brings him what's left of the blackened skull. Data says it has no power left in it. Dr. Crusher calls from sickbay to tell them Riker will be all right. Picard then contacts the Ferengi to tell them they are on a Federation mission and if any more Ferengi beam down to the planet (they have all since beamed up) it will be construed as an act of aggression. Zaeb demands to know what is going on with Riker, but Picard refuses to answer, adding that they do not have the skull. With that, the Ferengi break orbit and leave.

In sickbay, Riker awakens to see Picard, Troi, Worf and Dr. Crusher watching him. He apologizes, but Picard brushes the apology away, saying Riker's actions succeeded in sending the Ferengi away, peacefully.

Commentary: This is an old idea that has been done in many horror movies and books again and again. A crystal skull possessing its owner is a plot cliche. This episode, had it been made, would have been very weak. It is never addressed that Beverly was affected by the skull, and yet later seemed to forget about it. Also, Riker's behavior was so strange that I don't think Worf would have been so taken in.

However, if the actor had been subtle in his approach to the changes in his (Riker's) character, it might go unnoticed for a period of time. This episode might have had appeal, had it been made, to a younger audience, but older, more sophisticated Trek and science fiction fans would have had a lot of trouble with it. This kind of weak, cliche, unimaginative plot unfortunately dominates television episodic plots. I refuse to believe what some TV writers and producers believe, that the audience is just too stupid to notice or care. I believe TV viewers do care, and I, for one, am glad this one didn't get made.

## "DEAD ON MY FEET"

Story by Richard Krzemien (11-19-87)

Synopsis: The Enterprise pays a courtesy call to the planet Greater Tynen. Its world leader, Dennet Ownn, is a friend of Captain Picard's. But even though the world has a single leader, its government is considered to be very benevolent and democratic. Upon arriving at the planet, Picard is told that Ownn has died. The leader's second in command, Yarwick, invites Picard to the funeral. Picard, who is very upset by this turn of events, beams down with Dr. Crusher and a small Away Team.

The funeral is held in a huge crypt, but during the ceremony Dr. Crusher's instruments discover that none of the bodies there are dead, just in a deep coma. Medication is beamed down and all of the bodies are revived. The people are very grateful to be cured, with the single exception of Dennet Ownn.

Ownn explains that on Greater Tynen, when individuals no longer fill a useful role in society, their social status is terminated, their DNA purified and the genetic material returned to the society, which has somehow grown bland in the DNA department. Ownn fit into this category because a majority of the people no longer felt that his political views were in keeping with the mainstream. As a result of interfering with this, Picard and the Away Team are arrested, and they are sentenced to having their own social status terminated.

When Riker contacts the planet to find out why he hasn't heard anything from Capt. Picard, he's told that everyone on the Away Team is dead. When Riker beams down to view the bodies, he's informed that the crew members cannot be returned to the Enterprise because the genetic information in the bodies has been appropriated by the state and will soon be placed in the DNA bank.

Riker beams back to the Enterprise and contacts Starfleet to inform them of the situation. While awaiting a reply, he has the Transporter room lock onto the coordinates of the bodies of the Away Team. The Transporter room reports that sensors indicate that Picard and the others are still alive.

Riker beams down to confront Yarwick, and as he does he learns that the people Dr. Crusher revived have been beamed up to the Enterprise and taken control of the ship because Yarwick refuses to recognize the existence of these people. Arkis, the leader of the rebels, threatens to use the weapons of the Enterprise against the planet unless their social status is returned. Arkis orders Work to fire on the planet, but the Klingon refuses. After he is stunned with a phaser, Arkis discovers that no one else on the Enterprise will obey him either, and his people do not know how to operate the weapons systems.

When Ownn and Riker proved that Yarwick tampered with the voting results which had caused Ownn's social status to be removed, Yarwick is overthrown. While Yarwick has his own social status removed, Arkis and the others have theirs restored. When Picard and the others are revived, Ownn promises to work towards changing the laws which caused all this in order to redefine the meaning of what an individual can contribute to society.

Commentary: This plays much like an old sixties STAR TREK episode story. The idea behind it is good, though and could still be reworked into a future episode. What needed to be expanded on more is exactly how social status is defined. In the context of this story there is no such thing as the loyal opposition. Ownn was ousted supposedly because his political views didn't follow the majority. But on a planetary scale, would there ever really be a consensus? The fact that enough people would agree on one leader is the best anyone could ever hope for. What views did he hold which were supposedly rejected? The political elements of the story are a bit simplistic and ill defined. And how could the genetic material of the people have become "bland"? What does that even mean?

# "DEADWORLD"

Story by James Van Hise

Synopsis: The Enterprise picks up an important dignitary who has grown weak from an incurable withering disease and he wants to return to his homeworld to die. His presence disturbs some crew members as death on that alien world usually comes at the time of the individual's choice, and his suicide is surrounded by great ritual and celebration. Captain Picard was once stationed on that world and attended the suicide festival of a friend there.

Outsiders are sworn to secrecy regarding the arcane rituals of that planet, but Picard makes it clear to Riker that the experience changed his life, as well as his perception of life. Riker cannot accept it and whenever he deals with the dignitary his attitude is both cold and condescending.

Data is particularly fascinated by this alien dignitary. Since Data was not created the way ordinary beings are, he holds an unspoken fascination with what exists beyond the tenuous threshold of life. As the alien's disease becomes more advanced, he must eat in his room even though he had enjoyed exploring the ship and dining in the common area with the crew. He is aware that his presence has sparked some heated debates among crew members. The alien, although infirm, clearly takes great joy in living and seeing new things. He is not morbidly fascinated with death by any means.

Riker can't get over the fact that his captain was so moved by something on that world that be cannot by honor share with him. Finally Riker goes to the alien and tries to find out what could have so affected Picard. The alien replies enigmatically, "The truth."

Their discussions also deal with the fact that life should indeed be clung to, but not at the cost of the quality of life. Riker asks if there are ever group suicides and the alien recoils in horror at the thought, blurting out that, "To take someone with you when it was not their time and without the preparation of. . . it would consign the one responsible for taking someone against their will to unendurable oblivion—the oblivion of loneliness."

Riker explains that among his people, the person committing suicide will sometimes kill others before taking his own life in the belief that they will be together in death forever after. The alien shakes his head gravely, saying that such an action has the opposite effect. Riker leaves the conversation with much to think about but few answers.

Data arranges to deliver a specially prepared meal to the alien and he enters the dignitary's quarters so quietly that he witnesses something he was not meant to see—the alien in a trance-like state with an ethereal, transparent outline of another alien embraces him. The alien looks up and asks Data to please close the door. "You who question the nature of your own existence can best profit by the truth." The door closes.

The Enterprise reaches the planet and as the alien is prepared to beam down, Picard announces that he has been asked to accompany the dignitary to the surface for his ceremony, and he wants Riker to come with him. "It's something I want to share with you, Number One. It's something few beings who live outside the 'deathworld,' as you call it, ever learn in their lifetimes." They beam down and when they leave, Data overhears some crewmen talking about what a grim mission this has been. Data replies, "You couldn't be more wrong," and then walks away, whistling. No one has ever heard Data whistle before. It's a strange, buoyant yet alien tune.

On the planet's surface, the ceremony takes place and Picard and Riker are ushered into the private chamber where they put on special metallic ceremonial robes. The doors are sealed and the alien is placed on cushions where he lies flat, closes his eyes and wills his life to end spontaneously.

Picard and Riker actually see the image of the alien's life-force rise from his body, and as it does the room is suddenly filled with other such images of other aliens—the friends that have passed over before and have now come to accompany the being into the next stage of his existence. The metallic robes the watchers wear protects them from the strange energies unleashed when the departed aliens materialize. They observers watch in silence as the aliens greet the dignitary and then fade away into the next state of existence.

"That's what death is?" asks Riker.

"It is for them," Picard answers.

"What about for us?" Riker wonders.

"No man can say, Number One, but we can hope. Whatever is on the other side, it's like nothing that anyone has ever imagined."

Commentary: I wrote this in 1987 at the behest of a mutual friend of Gerd Oswald. Oswald had directed a couple STAR TREK episodes in the sixties and I'd spoken to him while he was directing an episode of the new TWILIGHT ZONE for CBS when I visited that studio in 1986. Oswald was looking for a story he could take to Paramount for THE NEXT GENERATION which he could attach himself to as the director. He read this outline but rejected it as being "too depressing." I told my friend that Gerd, who was then in his seventies, was obviously a man who had never come to terms with his own mortality. Gerd Oswald died two years later of cancer.

## "THE HANDS OF TIME"

Story by Ken Glidin

Synopsis: The deflector screens on the Enterprise come on automatically as though in response to a threat to the ship, but no threat can be ascertained. Troi states that she felt great joy before the screens sprang up, but this doesn't make any sense either. As a precaution, Picard puts the Enterprise on red alert status.

The computer reveals that it responded to a threat which appeared and disappeared so quickly that it was unable to determine its exact nature. An examination of log tapes by still-framing the visual record reveals two alien vessels. One of the vessels reappears but they are unable to communicate with it. Data explains that the language, which is comprised of clicking sounds, is based on the use of time intervals.

When the language is finally translated, it reveals the aliens to be the Caldendrians, a race capable of moving easily through time. The aliens are playing a form of time-tag and declare themselves non-hostile. When another vessel appears and "tags" the first ship with a time-ray, causing both to disappear, parts of the Enterprise disappear as well, taking 300 people with it! And Picard discovers that Riker is among the missing.

In the areas of the ship which connect to the vanished sections, a murky barrier is found beyond which there is nothing. Picard believes that the other sections of the Enterprise may be in a different time period. The aliens had revealed they were moving through a period equivalent to two Earth days. Data points out that since they don't remember anything about this from the recent past, then the missing sections must be somewhere in the near future.

Data suggest that perhaps they can rig the Transporter to be a time beam, and Wesley figures out how to do it. The transport beam could be dangerous, and Data volunteers believing he has the best chance of survival. However, in the Transporter room, Deanna Troi is already preparing to try it herself due to her concern over Will Riker.

Troi arrives in the missing section and finds dead crewmen, including Riker. She obtains the ship's log from there and returns to the main part of the Enterprise. The log reveals that the damage they witnessed was caused by the Ferengi. Because this will happen in the future, it may be possible to avert the tragedy.

Since the nacelles are among the missing sections, the Enterprise only has impulse power to maneuver with. But their awareness of the coming attack gives them an advantage. They use the ship's power to ready the shields and the phasers. A day and a half of waiting is rewarded when a Ferengi ship appears which has a Caldendrian ship held in a tractor beam as they are determined to learn the secret of the time ray.

The Ferengi open fire on the Enterprise. Simultaneously the Caldendrians send out a signal which reveals a weakness in the Ferengi tractor beam, which Picard fires at. The Caldendrian ship is freed and uses its time beam to send the Ferengi ship into the future. Then the second Calendrian ship appears and they use their devices to restore the missing sections of the Enterprise. The Calendrians, which had never contacted the Federation before, state that they will consider joining sometime in the future.

When Riker returns to the bridge, he doesn't even realize that he's been missing for two days or that he was even "dead" at one point.

Commentary: A routine adventure story, equal to some of the average mindless adventure episodes TNG has done. It's not bad but is awfully contrived. Troi's using the time beam, instead of Data, doesn't make a lot of sense, but at this early point in the series when this plot was composed, they were going to establish a relationship between her and Riker.

This story was also written at a time when the Ferengi were being groomed to be the black hats in the new series, but it never worked. These four foot tall aliens just never really managed to project danger and menace, and the entire race put together didn't even have the personality of one Dr. Loveless (as seen in the old WILD WILD WEST series).

## "THE IMMUNITY SYNDROME"

written by JD Kurtz

Synopsis: The S.S. Beagle drifting. The captain's log states that they are dying and death is their only hope for freedom. He orders all ship's hatches to be blown. From exterior view, this happens, and the atmosphere on the ship is released into the void.

Coincidentally, the Enterprise was en route to bring supplies to the Beagle when all contact is lost. The Enterprise launches a probe which determines, before they arrive, that the vessel is dead. When Picard arrives on the bridge, Riker informs him that the death of the ship is a mystery. There is no damage or radiation. Picard orders an Away Team to investigate. On the team are Riker, Dr. Crusher, her assistant Ames, Geordi and Data.

They beam over to the ship and immediately find a body frozen to a chair. Geordi tries to bring the ship's engines on line while Data inspects the computer. The computer is frozen, along with its entire memory, so they can learn nothing from it. They then receive communication from Crusher to come to the sickbay.

Life support is on and Crusher and her assistant remove their helmets. She leads Riker to a frozen body whose chest has exploded. The doctor thinks it is a result of the hatches being blown but tells Riker to stay away from it because there is a risk of contamination. She thinks the hatches were blown to destroy something that the Beagle couldn't control or fight.

The Away Team returns to the Enterprise and decontaminates. Bodies for autopsies are taken to sickbay. Ames looks sick but gives the excuse that he is just affected by the deaths of the people on the Beagle. Beverly orders him to sickbay, too.

In the ready room, Picard and Riker discuss why they didn't find bodies for the entire crew on board the Beagle. They theorize that a party beamed down to some planet and brought back a disease. Then when they discovered this, they beamed back down to find a cure. They never returned. Now they must retrace the course the Beagle was on.

In sickbay, Beverly examines Ames but he seems all right. She tells him to return for a follow up exam in two days.

Geordi is still trying to locate the Beagle's exact course, while Dr. Crusher reports that the cause of death on the Beagle was the explosive decompression and nothing more. However, something caused the captain to order the hatches opened. Riker has no proof there was a disease, but believes that is the case. Beverly also comments on Ames, saying that he should be treated gently because he's having a hard time dealing with death. He is young, and Picard sees nothing abnormal about that reaction.

Wesley offers to play 'chess-droids' with Ames, but Ames is uninterested. He is emotional and anxious. He complains they're in the middle of nowhere and don't belong in space. "It's not meant to be." He thinks the fate of the Enterprise will be the same as the Beagle's. He tries to fight Wes, but other crewmen break it up. Wesley calls for a medic and for security.

Beverly re-examines Ames and finds his white blood cell count up. He is still behaving irrationally, so she calls for Troi.

Picard, Riker, Beverly and Troi hold a meeting in the lounge. The captain's temper flares when he finds out Troi has no answers about Ames mental condition. Beverly says Troi is doing everything she can. Riker starts to cough which concerns Beverly because he never gets sick. Picard now thinks something has been brought back from the Beagle. Troi protests, saying they were all decontaminated. But Beverly points out that you can't decontaminate for something you don't know exists. They decide to examine the Away Team for any symptoms. Geordi leaves Wesley in charge of finding the Beagle's last trajectory.

In sickbay, Beverly asks Riker what he had for breakfast and Riker cannot remember. Geordi answers trivial questions correctly and is dismissed. Riker is ordered to stay. He and other members of the Away Team are to be prepped for surgery. Beverly wants to perform a brain scan. Then Ames screams. He is in the midst of a massive coronary. Riker witnesses the doctor's attempts to save him.

In sickbay, Beverly has determined that the Beagle's captain had a brain infection that reduced his immunities. It eventually results in death. The virus was brought back to the Enterprise by the Away Team. The only way to find a cure is to find out where the crew of the Beagle contracted the virus. Beverly is a carrier now, showing no symptoms. Riker and Ames are the only two infected.

The trajectory of the Beagle has been confirmed. The Enterprise heads in that direction. In sickbay, Riker grows weak and paranoid. He believes they're all going to die. Another crew member screams as two security men hold him. He was trying to kill himself with a thermite grenade. They strap him down and Beverly tells Picard things will get worse.

The Enterprise makes orbit around Aldebaron IV, where the Beagle last visited. There are already 12 cases in sickbay. They're beginning to lose control over the situation. Riker tricks a med-tech into letting him loose.

On Aldebaron, a man-made nuclear power source is detected. An Away Team is dispatched to investigate. They find a research hut with three bodies in it. They are the missing crew members of the Beagle. Meanwhile, the med-tech on the Enterprise informs Tasha that Riker is on the loose. The scene switches to show that Riker has obtained a phaser and is moving through the ship.

On Aldebaron, Beverly studies the left behind research and determines that a cure was found, but the Beagle didn't have time to use it.

On the Enterprise, Riker takes over auxiliary control. Geordi begins receiving an alert that auxiliary control has been locked off. He cannot override. Picard goes to auxiliary control and pleads with Riker to let him in. Riker will not, stating they are all dying and he just wants to help matters by speeding up the process. Picard demands that an engineer blow the door open, but when the engineer protests that sensitive equipment inside will be damaged, Picard pushes him against the wall and demands he follow orders. When he realizes he is out of control, Picard rescinds his order and they decide to cut through the door.

On the planet, Beverly is succumbing to the disease. She yells at Data, telling him he thinks he is superior to humans. She regains her senses enough to communicate to Data that she has finished her experiment. He takes a vial of green liquid and injects some of it into her. She collapses. When she comes to, blood samples indicate the vaccine worked.

When she contacts the Enterprise, however, things are bad. Orbit is decaying because Riker has control of the ship and is sending it crashing to the planet. Picard orders Beverly and Data beamed up. Wesley has come up with some kind of plan to sling-shot the Enterprise across the planet so they will not break up and will be able to break orbit. Picard implements the plan. It works. Then Riker, having been extricated from auxiliary control, pushes onto the bridge and demands he be arrested for mutiny. Beverly and Data escort him off the bridge and to sickbay.

Later, Picard congratulates Wesley. Geordi reports all engines back to normal. And the Enterprise engages warp and leaves the sector.

Commentary: The title is from classic Trek. But all that aside, the episode is nearly a word for word, scene by scene, plagiarism of "The Naked Time" by John Black. It appears that this treatment was intended to be a remake of "The Naked Time" and perhaps submitted before "The Naked Now" was filmed or shown. I think it's a mistake to remake old episodes into newer versions of themselves, even if the episode is a good one. It shows a lack of imagination, not only plotwise, but in characterization as well. "The Naked Now" is a weak script because of that. This one would have been just as bad. What a waste of time when there's a whole universe out there to explore. No remakes, please!

# "THE LEGACY"

Story by Paul Aratow

Synopsis: The Enterprise begins picking up a strange broadcast of recorded music which is suddenly interrupted when it receives a distress call from a passenger craft in trouble in a region reputed to be the "Bermuda Triangle of space." The Enterprise responds but is unable to effect rescue due to an ion storm in the region. A shuttle pilot named Lara volunteers to fly to the ship, but after she does both the shuttle and the passenger ship vanish from the scanners.

The shuttle just as mysteriously reappears and Lara reveals that she saw a beautiful winged creature outside her shuttle. Dr. Crusher determines that Lara is not suffering from hallucinations.

Other Federation ships then pick up a distress call from the Enterprise and radio that they are responding. The Enterprise picks up the strange recorded music again and Lara has a strange hypnotic response to it. Communications channels are jammed and the Enterprise cannot alert the approaching vessels to the danger that awaits them. To further confound everyone, Dr. Crusher reveals that Lara is pregnant with a rapidly developing fetus which wasn't present before she took the shuttle into that mysterious region of space. The child is affecting Lara by causing her to display fantastic powers.

Picard is able to get through to Starfleet and apprise them of the situation. Starfleet states that it may be necessary to perform an abortion on Lara. Lara warns Picard that the Enterprise must change course or else it will be in deadly danger. Picard is suspicious, believing that they are being tricked by the alien fetus. But Lara convinces the navigator to listen to her and the Enterprise narrowly averts disaster by changing course just in time.

Lara explains that the fetus is an alien child who is coming into the world to tip the balance in a positive way. Although Starfleet had ordered The Enterprise to perform an abortion on Lara, Picard refuses, allowing Lara to make the decision. She chooses to take a shuttlecraft back into the hole in space so that she can give birth in the parallel universe.

Commentary: An odd story which would have needed a lot of work. Since this was proposed during Roddenberry's more direct involvement with THE NEXT GENERATION, the abortion angle would have killed it for sure. No doubt in the future of STAR TREK, abortion would have been replaced by a process in which the fetus is removed from a mother who doesn't want to deliver a baby and either implanted in another woman or in an artificial womb.

Abortion purely for the purposes of murder is not at all in keeping with the rosy 24th century envisioned by Roddenberry. Plus this plot is pretty undeveloped, not to mention fairly mindless. We only have Lara's word that she isn't carrying the Anti-Christ or its equivalent. Lots of questions remain unanswered.

# "THE LOST AND THE LURKING"

Story by Robert Wesley

Synopsis: The Enterprise pops out of the mouth of the Dream Park which is orbiting one of the moons of Yensid. Miles across, the amusement station is in the shape of a gigantic mouse head with giant turning wheels in its ears and a landing bay in its mouth. The trajectory of The Enterprise sends it deep into an asteroid belt.

Capt. Picard is restless. He spent longer on the pleasure station than he'd intended, but if he hadn't he'd have had to have left with less than a full ship's compliment. The pressures of confinement, even aboard a ship as large as The Enterprise, are subtle and every few months the crew needs a change of scenery, whether it be shore leave on a planet or on one of the remote pleasure stations.

Picard and Riker are discussing the nature of pleasure and relaxation when a ship is detected. It's floating dead in space, or at least appeared to be until they approached, whereupon the ship began to parallel the course of The Enterprise.

"Registry, Number One?" Picard asks.

"The computer indicates that it's a free-spacer, a scavenger, numbers 00-973-5309850-111112. It also goes under the name of the Near Paranoia."

"Is that supposed to be a joke?" Picard asks.

"I'm not sure," Riker replies. "It's apparently a pretty notorious ship and hasn't checked in at any bases in months. In fact it was reported overdue from its logged in destination."

Communications attempts to raise the ship but they get only static mixed with something that sounds like screaming. The bridge crew are uneasy. Riker watches the ship on the screen and turns up the gain on the speaker. The screams sound pleading but the static drowns out the words.

"Where's the static coming from?" Picard asks.

"Interference is from inside the Near Paranoia."

"Inside? Maybe they're transporting something that's disrupted their broadcast bands. Data, where did the ship come from most recently?"

"The course indicates a possible rendezvous with a previously uncharted comet passing through the far side of this planetary system."

"Composition of comet?"

"Spectrascope analysis records common ice, nickel, iron but also one unidentified color band. Element unknown. Later log entries indicate that the Near Paranoia had staked out first claims on the comet due to proximity when the comet path had inexplicably shifted in that vessel's direction."

"Comets cannot abruptly change course," Picard states.

"This one did," Data responds.

"Looks like they made a find," says Riker.

"But did they find something or did something find them?" Picard wonders.

Garbled screams come across the speaker.

The Enterprise beams an Away Team over to the other ship, but the team is encased inside a protective force envelope. The Away Team consists of Riker, Mache Hernandez, Deanna Troi and Dr. Crusher. Inside the Near Paranoia, life support systems have been powered down to the bare minimum. They walk down the hall leading away from the deserted bridge. Data has opted to remain behind and scan the memory banks of the ship's computer.

The other three walk down a hallway while looking cautiously around them. Hernandez seems prepared for something to happen. Just then a figure falls from the ceiling right on top of Hernandez, pinning her to the floor so that she can't draw her sidearm. As they struggle, Riker calls out, "Don't hurt him! It's Rock, the ship's commander!"

The figure struggling with Hernandez isn't attacking her but rather is trying to just get her attention and also it seems to be trying to establish that Hernandez is <u>real</u>. Finally, as Hernandez gets a grip on it, Captain Rock screams into her face, "Scrape us off the wall!! For God's sake scrape us off the wall!!" He then buries his head in her arms and sobs helplessly.

Hernandez turns the man over to Dr. Crusher to examine. When he's been cleared by the doctor, he's to be beamed aboard the Enterprise to sickbay. As Riker and the security chief continue down the corridor, they come to the crew's common area and he plants the control by the door. They step through into darkness and Crusher finds the light stud and presses it, but before the level of light achieves more than twilight, she suddenly releases it and steps back.

A dozen men and women fill the lounge, or rather are part of it. To their left, half a man extends from a bulkhead. Above them a woman is pressed face first into the ceiling. Three others seem melted into the floor. But that's not the worst. A man and woman in front of them are somehow fused together, face to face.

Crusher scans the room with her med scanner and reveals to a shocked Riker that none of these people are dead. They approach the man fused into the wall and Riker reaches out and touches him. The man rotates within the bulkhead and turns towards the Away Team. His eyes open. Riker and Crusher back up involuntarily and bump into the man and woman who had been fused together—the woman is rotating within the man until they are both facing in the same direction, but still seemingly part of one body. "Poor Captain Rock," they say in unison, "he never did know how to have a good time." As the fused duo speaks, their skin and clothes ripple and flutter as though in a wind.

The crew of the Near Paranoia explain that they had entered the corona of the comet and encountered something that changed them, that transformed their bodies and made them impervious to the rigors of space. Rock had somehow been unaffected and when the ship left the comet, the crew found that they were able to slip between molecules and their bodies could not be harmed. They would also slip into trances where they could mentally see into parallel worlds. But it's clear that they have lost all touch with their humanity and their former personalities.

Riker and Crusher leave the people alone when they turn away from them. The people grow bored talking to normal humans.

Riker and Crusher talk about what's happened and what they can do about it. Then they encounter another crewman, someone who was only partially affected. He's seen things that frighten him, things from the "other side." This man, Ensign Kerry Gammill, knows that there is even more to this than meets the eye. The Near Paranoia's crew is planning to be picked up and taken to a colony so that it can infect more people.

One of the crewmen of the Near Paranoia enters the Transporter room and beams himself across to The Enterprise. He is looking for Capt. Rock. He finds him in the Sickbay and finally manages to infect him with what was in the comet. The two of them are discovered by Wesley Crusher. They are about to infect Wesley when Ensign Gammill bursts in. He can sense what the others are thinking as he is only partially controlled. They fight and Wesley escapes. He goes to the Transporter, locks in on sickbay and beams the combatants back to the Near Paranoia.

Data has examined the computer records and the sleeping members of the crew and has discerned that disaster is close at hand. Riker, Nattier and Data beam back to The Enterprise where Dr. Crusher had already returned and they put up their shields to prevent anyone else from beaming aboard. They discuss with Data whether there is anything they can do, but he replies in the negative. While they are conversing with Gammill on the intership communications, he begins to convulse. The infected crew of the Near Paranoia is dying as the organism that gave them peculiar abilities was using up the host bodies in the process. They needed new hosts, which the Enterprise crew have denied them.

Picard wonders if there isn't some way to communicate with the organisms through their hosts, but Data explains that there isn't time to learn how. Perhaps they didn't understand that they were inhabiting another intelligent organism, Riker wonders.

Aboard the Near Paranoia, strange voices are heard wondering whether they could now communicate with the other beings who are like their former hosts. There is no time, another replies, for they have no additional hosts available and their only means of survival was trapped inside the comet. The voices fade, in sadness and in pain.

Commentary: A strange first contact story. The opening with what looks like a planet-sized Disneyland seems to indicate an interest in exploring the idea of man's need for pleasure and sensory stimulus. This is touched on somewhat by the possessed crewman who remarks that Capt. Rock, "Never did know how to have a good time." Perhaps in a script this would have been explored more as the crew of the Near Paranoia (a great name for a ship) seems to be enjoying their possession.

That possession aspect is something like "This Side of Paradise" except that in the earlier story the possession was benevolent. The protective force envelope the Away Team uses seems to disappear without explanation as Mache Hernandez is jumped by Capt. Rock and knocked down. The existence in the story of Hernandez dates this as being a very early story treatment as Hernandez was an early version of Tasha Yar. Both were the security chief, but Hernandez was a rather obvious imitation of one of the characters in the 1986 movie ALIENS and so she was changed. Hernandez still exists, though, in the earliest series outline for ST-TNG.

# "THE MAY FLY"

Story by Richard Krzemien (10-1-87)

Synopsis: The Enterprise encounters an alien vessel which is commanded by an android. This android clones cells into beings which it trains to be guinea pigs for its experiments. In this case it is experimenting in sending human beings down to the surface of a planet which cannot support oxygen-based life. The androids believes that these clones are not true people and thus has no compunction about performing experiments with them which can only result in certain death.

An Away Team briefly visits the alien ship and encounters these cloned beings which have been trained to be completely fearless, no matter what they are up against, including whatever threat might be posed by the Enterprise and its weapons. When apprised of this further information, Picard decides that the android must somehow be convinced of a flaw in the reasoning behind its experiments. Picard realizes that since the clones do not fear death, neither do they respect life. Picard convinces the android that were the clones to understand the value of life they could contribute more to the experiments.

Commentary: An idea in keeping with the more philosophical bent of THE NEXT GENERATION. The idea of human beings used in experiments also brings to mind the Concentration Camp experiments of the Nazis of World War Two, which opens up other angles to pursue in the storyline. A very dramatic idea and actually a bit shocking—perhaps too shocking for THE NEXT GENERATION to pursue with the "G" rated television audience it always seems to have uppermost in mind.

## "THE NEUTRAL ZONE"

written by Greg Strangis

Synopsis: Commander Billings, chief of security from Starfleet Command, is due to arrive on the Enterprise. No one knows the reasons, but Tasha Yar is excited. Billings is a security expert and once taught at the Academy where he was highly admired by students and peers. However, for the last few years, Billings has avoided public scrutiny. His life has become a mystery.

The Enterprise has a rendezvous with the starcruiser Washington where Billings is stationed. For some reason, he refuses to transport over and insists instead on taking a shuttle. When the crew finally meets him in the shuttle bay, they are surprised to see that he is confined to an anti-grav wheelchair. No one knew he was so disabled.

Billings, about 40 years of age, is quite energetic despite his disability. Tasha asks if he will need special facilities and he replies that he does not. Wesley hangs around asking one too many questions about the 'chair', obviously fascinated with technology that is different. Irritated, Billings asks Picard why a boy is allowed on the bridge.

Picard ignores the question, and asks Billings what their mission is. Billings will not tell him, though he reveals that everything will be known to them soon. He leaves, with Tasha, to tour security stations on the Enterprise. Meanwhile, Riker, Geordi, Worf and Picard determine that their current heading will lead them into the Romulan Neutral Zone. Picard is concerned. Worf is ready for a fight.

On the battle bridge, Billings quizzes Tasha about various aspects of Enterprise security. He discusses Romulans with her, and wants to know who, if anyone, on board has ever had contact with them. She agrees to check computer records. Tasha then speaks to him of Davana VII (the world she's from) and he seems to know nothing of it. This hurts her but she says nothing, and initiates the standard computer search.

Dr. Beverly Crusher is (coincidentally) working on an experiment involving organ regeneration. Data visits sickbay to assist and they discuss Data's alien form, how it defies medical and scientific standards, and should not be able to exist. Data says the important thing is that he does exist, not how. (??? How very unscientific.) Meanwhile, Tasha and Billings have come up with a list of people who must be dropped off at the next starbase.

Picard is infuriated to discover Worf's name on the list. Picard stands up for his crew, and tells Billings that none of them will be excluded from this mission. He trusts them and wants them on the Enterprise with him. But, he compromises about Worf, assigning him duties away from the bridge, duties which include becoming Wesley's tutor. Billings is not happy, but accepts Picard's decision.

Then Picard orders Billings into his ready room where he demands that the man tell him what is going on. Billings explains that the Enterprise will be a base of operations for an important trade conference which will include the Romulan Empire. This is a new step for both Federation and Empire, and there are people who want to see this conference fail. Therefore, security will be extra tight. His reasons for removing Worf from the ship were well-founded since he believes Worf to have a cultural prejudice against the Romulans.

Picard admits that he himself has no love for Romulans, and had, years earlier, battled a pair of Romulan Birds of Prey. Billings knows all about Picard, and states that the battle forced the Romulans to view Picard as a man of honor. They had actually requested Picard be present at the trade conference. Thus, the Enterprise was chosen as the 'location' for the conference.

In sickbay, Dr. Crusher gives Tasha advice on how to speak openly with someone about feelings you have for them that go beyond professional considerations. The doctor says that a direct approach is called for every time. Later, Dr. Crusher sees Billings in the turbolift and asks him why he has not reported to sickbay for a standard physical. Billings makes up some weak excuses and Crusher orders him to report for an examination.

Billings visits Tasha in security. Tasha tells him that because of him, she joined Starfleet and became involved with security. Billings had been the leader of the forces who rescued Tasha and others from her home planet Davana VII. She tells him she owes him a debt that can never be repaid. Billings doesn't seem at all moved or concerned. He states that mission was quite ordinary. He then chastises her for not running tighter security on the ship.

When he leaves, Tasha is shocked and hurt by his rudeness. Then Geordi and Wesley enter, complaining about being restricted from certain areas of the ship. She explains Billings' reasons, but Geordi and Wes are not satisfied.

Finally Billings submits to a medical exam. Dr. Crusher asks how he injured himself, but Billings does not wish to discuss it. She tells him about the organ regeneration experiments she and Data have been working on, wherein she would take nutrients from Data's spinal column and inject them into Billings. This might result in regeneration of damaged nerve endings. Billings is not interested. He says this is just another experiment which would get his hopes up, then dash them when it failed. He has accepted his situation and learned to live with it. As he leaves, Wesley enters and tells him that he thinks he can enhance Billings' wheelchair. Billings rudely states he doesn't need anyone's help, and abruptly leaves the room.

The Enterprise approaches the Neutral Zone. Riker notices that Tasha seems disturbed. He is about to speak with her when they detect a Romulan ship approaching. The ship goes to Yellow Alert. Billings is called to the bridge. As Billings arrives, the ship answers the Enterprise's hail. A Romulan security officer beams aboard, and Riker, Tasha and Data meet him in the Transporter room. He is sub-Commander Gar, and comments to them about their primitive Transporter. In the corridor, they all run into Wesley and Worf. Worf scowls and mutters a racial retort.

In Picard's ready room, Gar assures Picard that though most disagree with this conference, the Empire wants to follow through. Gar thinks it is a waste of time, but he is here to make sure the Romulan delegates are not threatened or harmed in any way.

Later, in sickbay, Dr. Crusher speaks to Tasha about her experiments. She wonders if Tasha might be able to convince Billings to participate. Tasha is still upset by Billings and states she doesn't know if she can, but she does agree to look over Crusher's information. Meanwhile, Gar is touring the Enterprise, analyzing its security.

Worf lectures Wesley on Klingon history in the ship's library. The lecture concentrates mostly on battles, and as he begins to tell about a Klingon-Romulan battle where, of course, the Klingons were victorious, Gar enters. He states that Klingon history is not a history about how things really happened. They argue, insult each other, and Worf ends the argument by pointing out that Romulan ships are of Klingon design, therefore Klingons must be superior. Gar turns away. He asks Riker if he can continue the tour alone. Riker hesitates, but Billings says that if the Enterprise is truly secure, then Gar cannot be a threat. As Gar leaves, Worf says, "How can someone look so much like a Vulcan, yet act like such a moron?"

Wesley is intent on improving Billings 'chair' with or without Billings' consent. But he needs restricted materials in restricted areas. He convinces Worf to help him. They go to the Transporter room, but are locked out. Wesley plays a recorded tape of Picard's voice rescinding the lock order, and the door opens. Wesley then beams Worf to a storage room. He sets the Transporter to automatically beam Worf back in five minutes. Then Worf reappears, arms filled with the items Wesley wanted.

Tasha tries to talk to Billings about Crusher's experiment. He figures out that Dr. Crusher asked her to do this and tells her that he has been avoiding talking to her because he believes that her gratitude toward him for saving her on Davana would be exaggerated by his handicap and therefore lead her to think of him along romantic lines. Tasha is again hurt, but decides that Billings is quite wise in his observations.

Gar arrives on the bridge just as a ship loaded with trade delegates hails the Enterprise. Gar has approved of security measures, and gives his okay to beam the delegates aboard. Data, Riker and Tasha go to the Transporter room to greet them. During beaming, the Transporter squawks as it begins to malfunction. On the bridge, Gar panics. Geordi quickly reroutes more power to the Transporter and the other ship is able to pull the delegates back intact. The delegates demand to know what is happening. Picard has no answers. Then, in the Transporter room, Data discovers a device in the console, removes it, studies it, and announces the Transporter has been sabotaged.

Wesley and Worf come forward and explain that they used the Transporter for their own purposes. They admit guilt for entering a restricted area, but maintain innocence in the sabotage of the Transporter. Gar continues to complain about the trade conference being a bad idea. Picard has no choice but to take Worf into custody while the investigation continues. Worf proclaims his innocence to Tasha, telling her that a Klingon would not stoop to such tactics for murder. Tasha believes him.

In the ready room, Gar demands to be sent back to his ship. Picard tells him he will do so as soon as the Transporter is repaired. Billings, still believing Worf is guilty, keeps harping on the fact that he wanted Worf removed from the ship in the first place. Then, Tasha calls in to the ready room and tells everyone to look toward the main viewscreen.

Tasha then tells them that she's kept video records of people entering all authorized and unauthorized areas of the ship. The viewscreen shows a video of Wes and Worf entering the Transporter room. Later, it shows Gar enter, remove a face panel on the Transporter and insert a foreign object. Tasha freezes the image.

Everyone faces Gar. Gar shrugs. He admits his guilt but justifies his actions by stating that cooperation between their people is a mistake. But, the trade conference continues unhindered. In security, Billings tells Tasha he's sorry he was so brusque with her. She remains cold and leaves. The incredible wonderchild Wesley then enters with new designs for an improved wheelchair for Billings. Billings it too filled with regret about Tasha to pay attention.

The trade conference is a success. Picard notes in his log that he hopes the Romulans will treat Gar with honor, allowing him to take his own life which is their form of 'death with honor'.

In sickbay, Billings approves of Wesley's wheelchair, telling him he thinks Federation researchers would have great interest in his design. Dr. Crusher wonders why Billings won't allow Wesley to build the first unit for him. Billings says he hoped he wouldn't need it, then agrees to go through with Dr. Crusher's experiment.

The next scene shows Billings and Data on adjoining tables with Dr. Crusher operating.

The Enterprise is on its way to meet Billings' ship when they get word of another emergency. They are to deliver dilithium crystals to a far-off starbase, and they immediately lay in a new course. Then Billings <u>walks</u> onto the bridge, using only a cane. Billings is deliriously happy and asks Tasha if she is free to join him for dinner. Picard gives Tasha permission to leave the bridge. Tasha has said nothing, but arm in arm, they leave the bridge. Just before the doors close, Picard says they'll be delayed in getting Billings back to his ship. Billings replies that there is no rush. The doors close.

Commentary: This episode was probably rejected for the simple fact that it is too predictable. There are no surprises at all. The fact that Gar sabotaged the Transporter is so obvious that one wonders why smart people like Picard and Tasha, et al, couldn't figure that one out. Especially since there are hints all along that Gar disapproves of the conference. Also, the fact that Dr. Crusher is working on organ regeneration experiments at the same time a disabled person comes aboard the Enterprise is just too contrived for words.

That the surgery was a success is even more amazing. What Federation researchers and hospitals couldn't do for Billings, Dr. Crusher could do easily. Granted, she had Data, a device no one off the Enterprise has access to, but it is still too simple a solution to a major problem. And I find it constantly amazing that young Wesley can come up with designs and devices that Federation researchers (some of whom probably have a Ph.D. or two) working full time haven't already tried.

The time frame is also bad. Wesley would have had to come up with the device in a matter of days or less. The fact that this treatment was rejected didn't keep them from using Wesley's incredible inventions (whether they become part of major Fed research or save the Enterprise) in many, many other episodes. That, too, is amazing. Though the characterization of Billings and Tasha is the strongest asset to this script, all in all, this episode just doesn't play.

# "THE ONE AND LONELY"

Story by Richard Krzemien (6-18-87)

Synopsis: The Enterprise detects a small object in space which turns out to be the body of a Russian cosmonaut from the 21st century. Believing the body deserves a more dignified fate, they beam it aboard. Only then is it discovered that the cosmonaut is still alive!

The cosmonaut had been part of an international mission involving the United States, the Russians and other nations following the end of the arms race. In 2015 they had been bound on a mission to Mars when they encountered an alien vessel which had offered to share its advanced technology. The crew had been divided on this offer, and the cosmonaut in particular feared a return to the arms race.

Finally, the aliens grew resentful of the cosmonaut and made an example of him by placing him in suspended animation and launching him into the future.

Data observes that aliens capable of time travel could have come from the future to sabotage that Earth-Mars mission as the unity of it was the precursor to Starfleet. Were Starfleet not to exist then the aliens would have a better chance to attack our galaxy in the 24th century as there would be no organized, unified resistance.

The Enterprise traces the point at which the cosmonaut was launched into the 24th century and follows it back to the past where they immediately encounter and battle the alien spacecraft. This battle takes place near a space station. Following the battle Picard beams over to the space station and broadcasts a speech to the people of Earth telling them that they can only benefit in the future by rejecting the aliens now.

The aliens are determined to destroy both the Enterprise and the cosmonaut, but they fail. The Enterprise returns to the future with the aliens and destroys the time travel mechanism.

Commentary: What a can of worms this would open. First the people of Earth would have evidence of their own future in the form of Picard. Plus Picard calls upon the nations of Earth to forego short-term goals for the long terms goals of a time in the future when none of them will even still be alive! Not a widely popular philosophy among the people of late 20th century Earth, nor I expect among those of early 21st century Earth either.

Plus, would Picard destroy the time travel technology without turning it over to the Federation, or is he making the decision on his own to deny this technology to the 24th century worlds of Starfleet? Even so, wouldn't someone else in this alien race have the plans for this device somewhere? Once a discovery is made, it's rather hard to suppress it when a planetary government has been putting it to use, as the aliens clearly must represent some planet which had launched them on this mission. Lots of problems with this story.

## "SEE SPOT RUN"

Story by Michael Halperin

Synopsis: The Enterprise is dispatched to the world of Procyon III. It had been settled by a group which had nearly extinguished the native population of creatures called Rookas. The panda-like Rookas which survived were trained by the settlers to do simple tasks.

When the Away Team, which includes Riker and Wesley, beams down, they encounter Delva, a fifteen year old colonist girl who is frightened, but not of the Away Team. Delva's parents are in town to attend an annual celebration so the Away Team goes to investigate while Wesley stays behind with Delva.

The Away Team arrives in town and observes that the settlers have moved out of the modern buildings into more simple ones. And their ceremony consists of a massive book-burning, although the one book which Riker is able to examine has blank pages. One of the colonists, an old man named Kort, has the Away Team accompany him to his home.

Delva explains to Wesley that a long time ago the people of the world revolted when they were almost destroyed by misused technology so that now illiteracy is prized and knowledge is condemned. Real books are forbidden and those which still exist are kept hidden. Suddenly the police raid the home, capturing Kort, Troi and Geordi while Riker, Tasha and Data escape. When they attempt to contact the Enterprise they find that their signal is being blocked somehow.

In hiding, Riker falls through a floor and finds a Rooka tending a library. The Rookas are intelligent enough to have learned to read and write from the colonists before the revolt against knowledge. But the Rookas keep this a secret to protect themselves.

When the prisoners are condemned to death, Riker breaks in and threatens to destroy the Memory Master, the only device which the colonists will accept knowledge from. One of the Rookas then steps forward and reads from a book of Federation codes which proclaims that people should have the freedoms of expression, worship and assembly. The people accept these truths and agree to change their ways. The story ends after the Away Team has returned to the Enterprise and a Rooka is beginning to teach children to read and write.

Commentary: Since this was conceived before THE NEXT GENERATION had determined its own directions, it reads much like an average storyline from Trek Classic. There's a lot of running, hiding and confrontations. It's also about an enclosed society which is changed by the intervention of the Federation, not unlike the way Capt. Kirk was always ignoring the existence of the Prime Directive. It has some good ideas, though, as the elevation of ignorance over knowledge could have produced some good intellectual interplay if it had been worked out in more detail. But since this storyline was written five years ago and no one has bothered to dust it off, chances are no one will.

## "SOMEWHEN"

written by Vanna Bonta

Synopsis: The Pliedes, a passenger ship, sends a distress signal which the Enterprise picks up. The signal comes from the Docleic Triad, a 'Bermuda Triangle' of outer space. Many ships have been lost in that area over the years. Data notes an ion storm passed through there recently, and the effect of the storm has possibly created "an electromagnetic waterspout" which can be dangerous to ships. Sensors reveal "spheres within spheres" which are rings made of energy. Should the Enterprise go on? Picard decides there is no choice.

The Pliedes must be rescued. On full alert, they plow ahead. Tasha notices that holodeck 1B is in use without authorization. Worf investigates but finds no one there. As he turns to leave, a light glows from within the holodeck. The scene within shows Tasha in a fashionable bathing suit attending a wild beach party.

Picard is determined to save the 1000 people aboard the Pliedes, and tells his crew that many ships have passed through the Triad intact. Still, the risk is great, and he is also affected by the fact that the next day will be the anniversary of Jack Crusher's death.

In her quarters, Beverly, too, is gazing at a hologram of her husband, remembering him and regretting that Wesley, who is reading nearby, never really got to know him.

Back on the bridge, the ship has just passed into the first "ring." Geordi picks up the U.S.S. Orion on scanners, a starship lost in the Triad ten years before. They see the ship before them, covered in a green glow. It does not respond to hails, nor will the tractor beam work on it. It is as if it isn't there. Then the Enterprise becomes surrounded by the green light, but Picard decides not to turn back.

At their posts, both Data and Geordi are approached by an ensign neither one recognizes. Data's memory holds knowledge of every crew member, yet this one is unfamiliar. She reminds Geordi of someone he knew and admired at the Academy, but things never worked out between them.

The Enterprise enters the next "ring" just as Beverly Crusher, in her quarters, faces eating her meal alone. She has prepared her dead husband's favorite foods and just as she's about to begin to eat, a male voice says "I have just the right wine to go along with that." Crusher looks up to see Jack, her husband, sitting at the table across from her. The scene continues with Beverly and Jack eating in a place that is like no room on board the Enterprise. Jack asks if she's sorry they never had children. She replies that her career and husband are enough to keep her busy.

Riker and Picard enter the ready room, with Data trailing behind. When Data finally enters, he sees Picard with a beard talking to Jack Crusher. They make a toast: to the Stargazer. When Data moves back onto the bridge, everything is normal. The ship enters the third "ring" and Geordi picks up two more vessels on scanners. They both glow red, as the Enterprise now glows, and he calls Picard and Riker onto the bridge. They come out of the ready room perfectly normal, much to Data's relief. The two ships to not respond to hails, nor are any life readings detected on board them.

Data theorizes that the Triad and "rings" are causing members of the crew to partially cease to exist. Picard does not understand. Data says that time is altered, and if they do not get to the Pliedes quickly, it will be lost. When the Enterprise passes into the fourth "ring", Picard disappears from the bridge altogether. The computer reports he's in a science lab, but he does not respond to communications. As the signal from the Pliedes begins to break up, Riker sends Data to retrieve Picard.

As Data walks the ships corridors, he sees Geordi with the strange ensign. Geordi is no longer blind. When Data steps into the science lab, the room becomes Picard's quarters on the Stargazer as seen in "The Battle." Picard is bearded and holds a glass of brandy. Data backs away. Picard follows and the beard disappears but the brandy glass remains in his hand.

Data tells Picard that he is needed on the bridge. When they arrive, the Pliedes is on the viewscreen. It and the Enterprise are surrounded by a blue glow. Data states that they must leave. But Picard will not sacrifice the lives on the Pliedes. Since the Enterprise picks up no life readings from the ship, Data concludes that the ship is in a different time dimension. It has ceased to exist and the Enterprise will, too, if they remain much longer. Unfortunately, another ion storm is approaching, which may block their way out.

Data and Beverly Crusher try to pick up life form readings on the Pliedes, but all they can detect are machines. Data says that is because machines remain constant, but people make choices and alter their lives by those choices. The idea that parallel universes can exist fills Beverly with wonder. She comments that she might exist somewhere else. Wesley says "it's more like 'somewhen'."

On the bridge, Picard leaves Riker in charge and exits. Geordi calls Riker captain. Things have changed again; now Riker is captain of the ship. Data, walking through a corridor, sees through a doorway that Tasha Yar, beaten and bloodied, is being condemned to death on her home planet. He moves on, encounters the real Tasha, then a third one who is a judge playing god with a prisoner. It appears to him that the time lines are coming together, affecting each other, and hurries to the turbolift. In other time flashes scenes depict Geordi with a family never having been a member of Starfleet. Also, Picard walks into the observatory lounge and meets with Jack and Beverly Crusher.

When Data and the real Picard reach the bridge, Riker is adamant about leaving. He says that if they don't leave now, the ion storm will destroy them. When Picard relents, systems respond incorrectly.

They use the ships they saw earlier (at Wesley's ingenious suggestion) as markers to lead them out. Data leaves the bridge to make more studies of the time alterations. As the Enterprise pulls out of the Triad, the parallel timelines begin to collapse. He sees an alternate Riker and Troi in love revert back to professional demeanors, etc.

As the Enterprise approaches the first "ring", Wesley disappears. A computer confirms that neither he nor Dr. Crusher are on board. It is believed that Dr. Crusher willed herself into an alternate timeline where her husband is alive. Picard orders the ship back into the Triad hoping they will reappear.

Time starts to alter again. Picard searches for the world/timeline where Beverly might be and finally finds her serving on the Stargazer with her husband. He tells her of her real life and with the help of Wesley, who fades in and out (because if his mother doesn't exist in this universe, he was never born) convinces her that "We love you" and to come back. Wes appears and disappears. He appears again and finally, mom and son lock gazes. She decides to chose her son's reality and Jack disappears and Wesley remains.

When they enter the bridge, Picard orders the ship to leave the Triad at top speed. With the screen on 'rear-view', they all safely watch the ion storm they've barely avoided pass by.

Commentary: I like this one. It needs rewriting to clarify certain decisions made by Picard that seem less than professional. When problems began with time, he should have ordered the ship out immediately. So, re-writing would have to show how they might chose to leave but, for some reason, cannot.

## "TERMINUS"

Story by Philip and Eugene Price

Revised by Robert Lewin and Dorothy Fontana

Synopsis: The Enterprise is on its way to Bynax II on a routine supply mission when Picard receives a distress call. Ty Norson, the commander of the Byrnax II station, proclaims that his base is in extreme danger, but the message is cut off before the nature of that danger can be communicated.

Capt. Picard orders the Enterprise to increase speed to reach Byrnax II as quickly as possible. Shortly thereafter an object is sighted on a course which appears will intersect the Enterprise. They raise shields and as the object approaches, tensions increase until Data suddenly smiles and they begins to laugh. He explains that the object means them no harm. It passes the Enterprise without incident. Data is at a loss to explain his uncharacteristic laughter, even though he keeps on smiling.

The passing object has outdistanced the Enterprise and seems on course for Byrnax II, but then bypasses it. When the Enterprise reaches Byrnax II, sensors indicate no life signs. An Away Team is dispatched to the planet's surface. Riker states that something catastrophic must have happened, Data insists that nothing is wrong. Finally, Geordi determines the colonists are underground, having been evacuated to there by Ty Norsen.

Norsen can't explain why he ordered them all into hiding, or how he was able to send a distress call before the planet was seemingly threatened by anything. As it turns out, the Away Team reveals no danger on the planet surface and the people return to their stations. But Data's earlier behavior remains just as inexplicable as Norsen's behavior is now.

The unidentified object returns and this time scans the planet. When Norsen insists the Enterprise protect him, the object promptly vanishes.

Data and Geordi begin tracking energy waves which Norsen had earlier forbidden them to investigate, these waves lead them to a duplicate of the object they keep encountering in space. But this one is on the surface of the planet. When Riker attempts to drill into the object to get a sample, it emits a protective force field which hurls everyone backwards. The people start returning to their hiding places until the threat this alien object represents can be determined.

The spare-born version of this object reappears and begins bombarding Byrnax II with gamma rays, which kill any people who hadn't sought shelter underground. The sole survivor on the surface is a man who had previously been stricken with a fever. He is beamed to sickbay, along with the still strangely acting Data. It's feared that he's suffering some sort of malfunction. When Data attempts to reprogram himself to rid his systems of whatever is interfering with his systems, he finds that he cannot get rid of whatever is in there. Although Wesley recommends that he speak to Dr. Crusher, Data refuses, and determines that for the good of the ship he should terminate himself.

When the others discover Data's plans, they plead with him, but Data feels responsible for the deaths on Bynax II and fears that he'll bring the same catastrophe to the Enterprise. Picard refuses to accept this and places Data under guard to prevent the android from harming himself. When Data reveals that guards could not prevent him from willing himself to die, Picard orders the sentries to tell him anything unusual that Data does, even if it's just the android closing its eyes.

When Wesley comes to see Data, the android closes his eyes, seemingly beginning his self-termination. Wesley begs him not to and even expresses love for the android. Data temporarily relents and states that he'd like to see the stars once more before his death. Wesley convinces the guards that Data is recovering so that he can take the android to Ten Forward. Then down on the surface of Bynax II, Riker encounters Data, who is supposed to be confined to his quarters on the Enterprise.

Wesley explains to Picard that Data somehow eluded him and the guard, as his desire to go to Ten Forward was only some sort of ruse. But the Transporter room computers indicate that no one has beamed down. Picard orders the Data that Riker has found put into restraints and beamed aboard the Enterprise.

On the Enterprise, Data awakens and learns that another Data has just been beamed aboard. Data, now in a weakened state, manages to return to his quarters where he encounters the second Data. Both Data's are brought to the bridge where they begin to unravel the mysteries.

The object on the planet's surface is a duplicate of the device which had created Data back on his native world. There are apparently many devices like this throughout the galaxy, and this particular one is on Bynax II to help make the planet habitable. One of these devices had been destroyed and the space-born version was dispatched to hunt down the people responsible but its programming got fouled up.

Instead, it started to search out human life forms in general to eliminate. Thus the device on the planet knew ahead of time that a faulty other version of itself was advancing on the planet and represented a threat to its inhabitants. It influenced Norsen's mind into making the people seek shelter. But when the threat couldn't be articulated, a duplicate of Data was created to explain the threat more directly.

In order to lure the defective object back, Wesley comes up with objects which give off human-like body readings to act as bait. Data II beams down with the devices, and when the space object returns, the Enterprise blasts it with a photon torpedo. Before the Enterprise leaves Bynax II, they see a viewscreen image of Norsen and Data III, yet another duplicate created by the machine in order to help the people safely inhabit that world.

Commentary: This was written before the full origin of Data had been worked out and established. Thus instead of Dr. Noonian Soong we have an alien machine which created Data, and which can create as many more of him as it wants. That this was an early first season outline is evidenced by Dorothy Fontana's involvement (she left the show by season's end) as well as by the penchant to have that boy genius Wesley come up with just what was needed in the climactic moment.

This aspect of Wesley was played down after many people began complaining about it since it was used as a crutch in the first season. This was because Roddenberry had created Wesley in his own image and wanted the character to be important. In 1988, at the Museum of Broadcasting event honoring him in Los Angeles, he seemed taken aback at the criticism of Wesley constantly saving the day, trying to explain that they just happened to use that in some scripts which were produced close together. What he couldn't explain was why it was thought an idea good enough to use more than once. Overall, "Terminus" is a fairly average story and actually better than some of the below-average entries filmed during the first season.

## "TWO YUFFS TWO MANY"

Story by Richard Krzemien (7-2-92)

Synopsis: The Enterprise meets with a number of other vessels in orbit around the Silonion M Cluster. The Enterprise is to serve as the meeting place for delegates who are to sign a peace treaty between two worlds which have been at war for generations over the disposition of a mineral called linignite. Aboard the enterprise, the delegates, Lek of Dryden and Theor of Alphus seem to be going out of their way to cause problems. They request certain refreshments which are beyond the capabilities of the food synthesizer to produce, and then act insulted when they can't get what they want. When Picard complains to Starfleet over the escalating demands of the delegates, he's told to placate them within reason and get the peace treaty signed.

A trading vessel shows up manned by two brothers, Zio and Dudney Yuff, who claim to have most anything that the delegates could want. Picard looks upon this as an answer to his delicate problems. But the Yuffs are governed by the profit motive even more than the Ferengi are. One of them even starts a fight between the two delegates just so that he can steal a locket from Lek's belt. The Yuffs are actually aboard the Enterprise to loot certain things from it and care nothing about disrupting the peace conference. One of them shape-shifts to look like Riker at one point in order to avoid detection. They even make themselves look like Lek and Theor in an effort to call off the peace conference.

After disguising himself as Picard to steal a tri-corder, the plans of the Yuffs begin to unravel as it becomes clear they can shape-shift. Picard puts the Enterprise on alert and orders the Yuff brothers found. Then a Ferengi ship is detected in the area. The Yuffs have been stealing things that the Ferengi want and are planning to reach designated coordinates so that the Ferengi will beam them off the Enterprise.

Lek manages to steal back the locket the Yuffs had stolen, revealing when he does so that it's a detonator. Lek had swallowed an explosive so that he could set it off should it look as though the peace talks are working. Lek declares his intent to blow up himself and the Enterprise. Dryden doesn't want peace, but wants to control all avenues of the linignite. Lek is beamed away just as he's about to detonate the explosive. Lek had been standing in the coordinates which the Yuffs were to be at to be retrieved by the Ferengi. No sooner does Lek appear aboard the Ferengi ship than it explodes.

The Yuffs admit that they had been hired by the Ferengi to disrupt the talks since the Ferengi had not been invited to participate. The peace treaty is signed and the Yuffs have been taken into custody by the Federation.

Commentary: Certainly complicated enough for a one hour story, but the peace conference aboard the Enterprise was already done in "Lonely Among Us" although it could be argued that this just establishes the tradition, just as "Journey To Babel" did on Trek Classic with the same idea. Much of the story comes across as though it were being played for laughs rather than being about a serious peace conference. The Ferengi appear and are used as the villains they were being groomed to be in 1987-88, although they never came off very well in that role after it was decided to make them five feet tall. One could say they never truly lived up to their stature as villains.

# EXCLUSIVE PREVIEW

*Rumors are spreading that THE NEXT GENERA-TION will end after the seventh season. What will come after THE NEXT GENERATION?*

# *DEEPSPACE NINE, FUTURE TREK*

January 1993 marks the launch of STAR TREK—DEEP SPACE NINE. Ironically this was announced shortly after the death of Gene Roddenberry. The timing led to speculation that if Roddenberry lived, this series wouldn't have. The description of the series helped fuel these suspicions. "It's going to be darker and grittier than THE NEXT GENERATION," executive producer Rick Berman stated in the March 6, 1992 ENTERTAINMENT WEEKLY. "The characters won't be squeaky clean."

What would Gene Roddenberry have thought of this? People close to him have stated that Gene hated STAR TREK VI because Enterprise crew members were anti-Klingon bigots. After all, in the future that Roddenberry made, humankind had outgrown such pettiness.

According to Rick Berman, DEEP SPACE NINE is not going to be his and executive producer Michael Piller's own personal take on STAR TREK. He insists that this will be just another way of expressing Gene Roddenberry's vision and will be fitting and consistent with everything that has been done with STAR TREK before.

## THE SETTING

The series is set aboard a space station in orbit around the planet Bajor. The Bajorans have been seen previously and are the same race as Ensign Ro. Ensign Ro was introduced in season four and became a semi-regular on THE NEXT GENERATION in season five. She was most prominently featured in the fifth season in the episode "The Next Phase." While Ensign Ro is an ex-terrorist who was drafted into Starfleet due to her expertise in certain matters, DEEP SPACE NINE will deal with a different aspect of the Bajorans.

The space station was established by the Cardassians and the Bajorans in conjunction with other alien races. As a result, it reflects cultural needs and biases often unfamiliar to some Starfleet personnel. The station was considered of remote interest until a fixed, stationary wormhole was discovered near the star system where Bajora is located. This wormhole, due to its non-fluctuating nature, can be explored and plotted. It's also discovered that it can be used as a gateway to a distant, unexplored quadrant of the galaxy.

Bajora has initially been described as a stripped mining planet, but one whose culture is very conscious of the spiritual and the mystical. The Bajorans even believe that the stationary wormhole was created through divine intervention because its existence a dying, backwater world. One of the regular characters will be a religious leader from Bajora who holds very strong views on the purpose of the wormhole.

Set in the year 2360 A.D., the new series is contemporary with THE NEXT GENERATION. While the extent of cross-overs between the two series have yet to be fully determined, STAR TREK—DEEP SPACE NINE will be launched with a two hour premiere and will include a stopover from the Enterprise and Jean-

Luc Picard. However, Starfleet personnel accustomed to the clean, modern conveniences of starship life will have to adjust to life aboard the space station which reportedly includes a casino and a holographic brothel as the space station also serves as a port of call for merchant ships.

## THE CHARACTERS

DEEP SPACE NINE is slated to feature seven or eight regular characters. The commander of the space station is a Starfleet captain who was serving with his wife on board one of the vessels attacked by Picard when he had been transformed into Locutus of Borg. The man's wife was killed in the attack and he had been rotated back to Earth in semi-retirement to recover from the ordeal. His command of the space station is his first active duty post since his wife was killed about three years before. Needless to say, he harbors some ill will towards Picard and finds it difficult to accept that Picard was *completely* helpless to stop the attack. Their meeting in the premiere episode will indeed be tense.

Another character is a shape-shifter security officer. This alien comes from a world on the other side of the wormhole, but does not remember his past. In order to fit in among the people he has encountered, he has chosen to adopt a humanoid form, but his efforts at maintaining this form are imperfect. The producers have stated that this character will be used to explore the nature of humanity and what truly defines one as being human. In this respect, he will occupy the position of Spock and Data.

Years before, the alien came out of the wormhole in a spacecraft and served the Cardassians on the space station. The alien is just as willing to assist Starfleet as he has aided the Cardassians. With Starfleet planning to explore the galaxy through the wormhole, he believes that he may at last uncover the clues he needs to unlock the secrets to his past. A shape shifter similar to this alien appeared in STAR TREK VI—THE UNDISCOVERED COUNTRY. Just as in that movie, the transformation effects will employ techniques pioneered in the movie TERMINATOR 2.

The science officer is a woman who uses a 24th century wheelchair to get around in the space station since she comes from a low gravity world. The other characters remain a secret, although the producers have hinted that they want to use a couple of characters who have appeared previously on THE NEXT GENERATION. These characters would be in supporting roles, not part of the main ensemble group of players.

Executive producer and series co-creator Michael Pillar has stated that it wouldn't be out of the question to see such characters as Q or Lwaxana Troi turn up on the series. This could also mean appearances by Klingons, Romulans and perhaps even the Borg. While the producers have revealed that the Enterprise and Captain Picard are definitely slated to appear in the premiere episode, how full the crew roster of the Enterprise will be in that story is still being negotiated.

## THE STORY BEHIND THE STORY

Even though the announcement about DEEP SPACE NINE seemed to come from nowhere several weeks after Roddenberry's death, Michael Piller and Rick Berman had been discussing ideas for a new series with Gene early in 1991. When Brandon Tarticoff moved from NBC to Paramount, he told Rick Berman that he wanted to see a spin-off from STAR TREK to launch into syndication. Berman and Piller returned to their series notes and worked up a proposal which Tarticoff approved.

The reason that Paramount wanted a new STAR TREK television series to run concurrent with THE NEXT GENERATION is that Paramount presently envisions ST—TNG lasting seven seasons, which will give the studio a healthy syndication package of about 170 episodes. DEEP SPACE NINE will run concurrent with the last year and a half of the first run episodes of NEXT GENERATION. This will serve to help establish DEEP SPACE NINE so that when THE NEXT GENERATION goes into reruns, a new and different STAR TREK series will already be established and in place in the syndication market.

By establishing DEEP SPACE NINE as being contemporary with THE NEXT GENERATION, even after TNG goes off the air, characters from that series could still turn up on the new series. THE NEXT GENERATION is slated to go into production as a new series of feature films once the seven season runs out. No doubt such a feature film would also include some sort of cross-over from DEEP SPACE NINE.

It's hard to believe that back in the seventies, many people were saying that STAR TREK was just old news and that nothing would ever be done with the premise again.

**PIONEER** **5715 N. Balsam Rd.   Las Vegas, NV 89130**

Pioneer Books wants to be your entertainment book company and make you happy by producing the best books we can about your favorite subjects. Your voice is important in choosing which books we publish. Please complete this questionairre and either photocopy it or tear it out and send it back to us.

Name _____    Age: 18-25___  26-35___  36-45___  45+___

Occupation _____    Education: High School____  College_____  Adv. Degree_____

Yearly Earnings: under $25,000___    $25,000-$50,000___    $50,000+__                Sex: male___ female___

Address: _____

How did you hear about our books?_____

Is your first Pioneer book?  yes___   no___   What Pioneer book(s) do you have?_____

Other than bookstores and mail order, where else would you like to be able to purchase our books (i.e. gift

shops, Walmart, Target, K-MART)?_____

Rate the book(s) on a scale of 1-5 (5 being the highest)_____

How could we make the book(s) better?_____

If you purchased the books, why did you buy the book(s) (ie gift, personal, job related)?_____

What publications do you subscribe to or read on a regular basis?_____

What are your favorite T.V. shows?_____

What other books would you like to see us publish?_____

Couch Potato carries a full line of Pioneer Books. Would you like to be added to the list to receive notice of upcoming new releases and a free catalog of all titles?  yes___   no___

Please add any other comments you may have:




THANK YOU VERY MUCH!

*David Marin*

ORDER TOLL-FREE **ANYTIME**
**800/444-2524** Ext. 67
Fax 813/753-9396

**The Lost In Space Technical Manual,** featuring technical diagrams to all of the spacecraft and devices, as well as exclusive production artwork.

Limited Edition:   $14.95

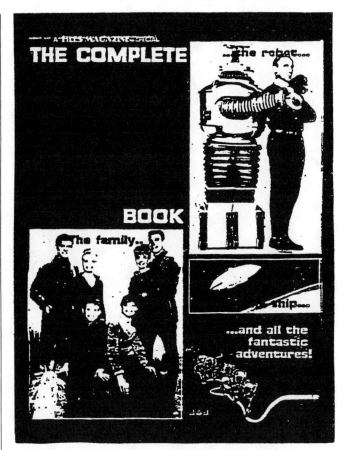

## THE COMPLETE LOST IN SPACE
Written by John Peel

The complete guide to every single episode of LOST IN SPACE including profiles of every cast member and character.

The most exhaustive book ever written about LOST IN SPACE.

$19.95...220 pages

Couch Potato Inc.          5715 N. Balsam          Las Vegas, NV 89130          (702)658-2090

**The Lost In Space Tribute Book** Written by James Van Hise
LOST IN SPACE remains television's second most popular science fiction series, only falling behind the legendary STAR TREK. The show began in 1965 and ran for five seasons, but has continued to live on in syndication ever since, with legions of fans clamoring for a reunion film.
Now, for the first time ever, Pioneer presents THE LOST IN SPACE TRIBUTE BOOK, the ultimate guide to this unique television series.
Author James Van Hise presents a guide to every episode aired during the series' run, plus exclusive interviews with the late Guy Williams, June Lockhart, Marta Kristen, Mark Goddard, Angela Cartwright, Bill Mumy, the Robot and, of course, Jonathan Harris, as well as various behind-the-scenes personnel. As a special bonus, the book features blueprint reproductions and a guide to the Jupiter 2 spacecraft.
$14.95.........164 pages
Color Cover, Black and White Interior Photographs, Blueprints and Charts
ISBN# 1-55698-226-7

"The first and only book of it's kind! The story of a new generation of adventures aboard the starship Enterprise. Star Trek fans and film students won't want to miss this one."
—Enterprise Incidents

# THE MAKING OF THE NEXT GENERATION

## BY EDWARD GROSS

# TREK
*The Next Generation*
**James Van Hise**

● The *Star Trek* phenomenon celebrates its 25th anniversary as the new television series enters its fifth season

T hey said it wouldn't last, and, after its cancellation in 1969, it looked as if it wouldn't. But the fans refused to let it die and now *Star Trek* is thriving as never before. The *Next Generation* television series—entering its fifth year—continues the adventure. This book reveals the complete story behind the new series, the development of each major character, and gives plans for the future.

**James Van Hise** is publisher editor of *Midnight Graffiti* and has written numerous books, including *The 25th Annniversary Lost in Space Tribute*.

*$14.95, Trade paper, ISBN 1-55698-305-0*
*Television, B&W photos, 164pp, 8⅜ x 10⅞*
**Pioneer Books**

**The Making Of The Next Generation**
Written by Edward Gross
Pioneer Books and the author of TREK: THE LOST YEARS, team up again to explore another untapped aspect of the STAR TREK universe, with THE MAKING OF THE NEXT GENERATION.
THE MAKING OF THE NEXT GENERATION provides a behind the scenes look at the first season of STAR TREK: THE NEXT GENERATION, featuring interviews with cast members Patrick Stewart, Jonathan Frakes, Brent Spiner, Levar Burton, Denise Crosby, Gates McFadden, Michael Dorn and Wil Wheaton, a set visit, interviews with such crewmembers as directors Paul Lynch and Joseph Scanlan and writers Dorothy Fontana, Richard Krzemien and Tracy Torme, as well as an examination of the metamorphosis that each script passed through on its journey from concept to aired episode.
$14.95.............132 pages
ISBN#1-55698-219-4

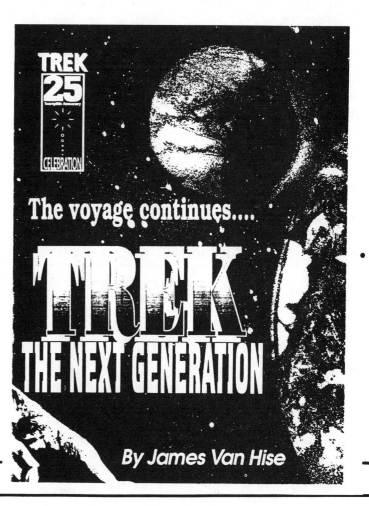

TREK 25 CELEBRATION

The voyage continues....

**TREK THE NEXT GENERATION**

*By James Van Hise*

# THE HISTORY OF TREK

*The Complete Story of Star Trek from Original Conception to its Effects on Millions of Lives Across the World*

**James Van Hise**

- *Star Trek VI*, the last Trek movie to star the original crew, will be released this winter
- By the author of *The Trek Crew Book* and *The Best of Enterprise Incidents: The Magazine for Star Trek Fans*

This book celebrates the 25th anniversary of the first "Star Trek" television episode and traces the history of the show that has become an enduring legend—even non-Trekkies can quote specific lines and characters from the original television series. *The History of Trek* chronicles "Star Trek" from its start in 1966 to its cancellation in 1969; discusses the lean years when "Star Trek" wasn't shown on television but legions of die-hard fans kept interest in it alive; covers the sequence of five successful movies (and includes the upcoming sixth one); and reviews "The Next Generation" television series, now entering its sixth season.

Perhaps no series in the history of television has had as much written about it as "Star Trek," but fans continue to snap up books and magazines about their favorite show. When the series first appeared on television in the 1960s, a book was already available chronicling its creation. And after the show was dropped three years later, people continued to write about it, actually increasing attention to the show until it returned in the form of a $40 million feature film in 1979.

Complete with photographs, *The History of Trek* reveals the origins of the first series in interviews with the original cast and creative staff. It also takes readers behind the scenes of all six Star Trek movies, offers a wealth of Star Trek trivia, and speculates on what the future may hold. A must for Trekkies, science fiction fans, and television and film buffs.

**James Van Hise** is the author of numerous books on entertainment, including *Batmania* and *The 25th Anniversary Lost in Space Tribute*. He lives in San Diego, CA.

*$14.95, Trade paper, ISBN 1-55698-309-3*
*Television/Film, 25 B&W photos, 160pp, 8⅜ x 10⅞*
**Pioneer Books**

# TWENTY-FIFTH ANNIVERSARY TREK TRIBUTE

**James Van Hise**

- The Star Trek phenomenon is celebrating its 25th anniversary
- Written by the author of *The Trek Crew Book* and *The Best of Enterprise Incidents: The Magazine for Star Trek Fans*

Taking a close-up look at the amazing Star Trek story, this book traces the history of the show that has become an enduring legend. James Van Hise chronicles the series from 1966 to its cancellation in 1969, through the years when only the fans kept it alive, and on to its unprecedented revival. He offers a look at its latter-day blossoming into an animated series, a sequence of five movies (with a sixth in preparation) that has grossed over $700 million, and the offshoot "The Next Generation" TV series, which will be entering its fifth season as Star Trek celebrates 25 years of trekking.

Complemented with a variety of photographs and graphics, the text traces the broken path back from cancellation, the revelation of the show's afterlife in conventions, and its triumphant return in the wide screen in *Star Trek: The Movie*. He also looks at such spin-off phenomena as the more than 100 Star Trek books in print—many of them bestsellers—and the 50 million video-cassettes on the market.

The author gives readers a tour of the memorials at the Smithsonian and the Movieland Wax Museums, lets them witness Leonard Nimoy get his star on the Hollywood Walk of Fame in 1985, and takes them behind the scenes of the motion-picture series and TV's "The Next Generation." The concluding section examines the future of Star Trek beyond its 25th anniversary.

**James Van Hise** who has authored such comics as *The Real Ghostbusters* and *Fright Night,* serves as publisher/editor of the highly acclaimed *Midnight Grafitti* and is the author of numerous nonfiction works, including *The Trek Crew Book, The Best of Enterprise Incidents, The Dark Shadows Tribute,* and *Batmania.* He lives in San Diego, CA.

*$14.95, Trade paper, ISBN 1-55698-290-9*
*TV/Movies, 50 B&W photos, line drawings, maps, and charts throughout, 196pp, 8⅜ x 10⅞*
**Pioneer Books**

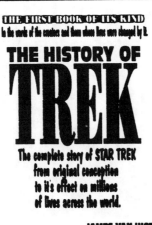

Couch Potato Inc.　　　　　Las Vegas, NV 89130

**The Trek Encyclopedia**
Written by John Peel
Everything you wanted to know about STAR TREK, but were afraid to ask!
THE TREK ENCYCLOPEDIA, as the title suggests, is a complete guide to the STAR TREK universe, providing descriptions, explanations and a breakdown of every character, alien race, monster, planet, space ship, weapon, technical devices and person who worked on the series, from the stars to the stunt doubles, and from extras to producers, directors, the make-up team to cameramen....all in alphabetical order.
Ever wonder who the first captain of the starship Enterprise was, or what the background of Khan Noonian Singh is, or where Mr. Spock hails from? These questions and countless others are answered, as the author provides the most detailed technical guide to STAR TREK *ever* presented.
$19.95..........372 pages
ISBN# 1-55698-205-4

## A STAR TREK CHRONOLOGY

**1964:** Gene Roddenberry produces the first STAR TREK TV pilot, "The Cage," starring Jeffrey Hunter as Captain Christopher Pike and Leonard Nimoy as the Vulcan, Mr. Spock. NBC rejects the pilo, but agrees to finance a second one.
**1965:** "Where No Man Has Gone Before," STAR TREK's second pilot, costarring Nimoy, but featuring William Shatner as Captain James T. Kirk. NBC is impressed, gives green-light for serie.
**1966-1969:** STAR TREK barely survives three seasons with mediocre ratings, but is saved from cancellation after year two by an unprecedented letter writing campaign. The plug is pulled in 1969.
**1970-1979:** THE LOST YEARS
**1979:** STAR TREK: THE MOTION PICTURE
**1982:** STAR TREK II: THE WRATH OF KHAN. The film is a tremendous success.
**1984:** Leonard Nimoy directs STAR TREK III: THE SEARCH FOR SPOCK.
**1986:** 20th Anniversary of oritinal show. STAR TREK IV: THE VOYAGE HOME. Announcement of THE NEXT GENERATION.
**1987:** STAR TREK: THE NEXT GENERATION premieres in October.
**1989:** William Shatner directorial debut on STAR TREK V: THE FINAL FRONTIER

"An essential book for STAR TREK fans..."
Enterprise Incidents

THE TREK ENCYCLOPEDIA
NOW INCLUDING PLANETS, SHIPS AND DEVICES
BY JOHN PEEL
A UNIQUE REFERENCE
TO EVERY ACTOR, DIRECTOR AND WRITER
TO WORK ON THE SERIES
PLUS COMPLETE DETAILS
ON EACH OF THE CHARACTERS
AND ALIEN RACES
AND MUCH, MUCH MORE!
EDITED BY HAL SCHUSTER

**The Wild Wild West Book**
Written by James Van Hise
When James Bond hit in the 1960s, television take-offs, from GET SMART to THE MAN FROM U.N.C.L.E., followed.
THE WILD WILD WEST was a bizarre, highly effective hybrid of two genres: the Western and the spy adventure, resulting in one of the most imaginative series ever broadcast, chronicling the exploits of James West and Artemus Gordon against the forces of evil. It has been copied ever since
THE WILD WILD WEST BOOK profiles stars Robert Conrad and Ross Martin and presents a complete episode guide, as well as a look at the show's various gadgets and disguises, super-natural elements and the novels and comic books. WILD WILD WEST fandom is also examined along with the reunion films, THE WILD WILD WEST REVISITED and MORE WILD WILD WEST.
$14.95.................124 pages Black & White Photos
ISBN#1-55698-162-7

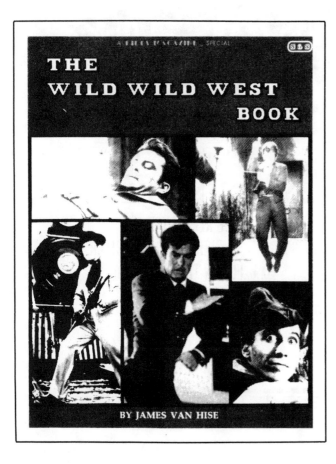

**Who Was That Masked Man?**
**The Legend of the Lone Ranger**
Written by James Van Hise
The Lone Ranger is a part of the national conscience, a legend handed down from generation to generation. Like all classic Westerns, the tales of the Masked Man and his faithful Indian companion, Tonto, are told with clear-cut definitions of right and wrong.
The Lone Ranger is one of a handful of characters who successfully trascends entertainment mediums, a radio "star," the subject of movie serials, hero of a weekly television series, motion pictures and currently headed back to both television and the movie screen with brand new productions for 1990.
WHO WAS THAT MASKED MAN? is a complete history of the character's exploits, examining his continued success and providing a guide to his comic book and filmed exploits.
$14.95..........148 pages
Cover Photo, Black and White Interior Photos
ISBN#1-55698-227-5

Couch Potato Inc.          5715 N. Balsam          Las Vegas, NV 89130          (702)658-2090

the behind-the-scenes story
exclusive interviews with the writers and directors
a complete guide to every episode ever aired

The longest running network television drama ever!

GUNSMOKE
YEARS

JHN PEEL

**The Gunsmoke Years**

Written by John Peel

Television's longest running series and most beloved Western is brought to life in this loving tribute that looks at 22 year of television history.

The text, written by the author of THE TREK ENCYCLOPEDIA, provides interviews with personnel from the show, character profiles and an episode guide to all 22 seasons.

THE GUNSMOKE YEARS is the first book *ever* devoted to GUNSMOKE, and the final word on the subject.

$14.95.........216 pagesColor Covers Black and White Interior Photos

*ISBN#- 1-55698-221-6*

# ORDERING INFORMATION

Use any major credit card and order toll free any time day or night by calling (800) 444-2524 ext 67. Or, send check or money order to Couch Potato, Inc. 5715 N Balsam Rd. Las Vegas, NV. 89130 (order coupon is on following page).

## Shipping:

If ordering by mail, include $3.25 s/h for the first book and $2.00 for each additional book. Please allow 2 to 3 weeks for delivery although we are usually much faster.

## Special UPS 2 Day Rush Service:

Special Service is available for desperate Couch Potatoes. These books are shipped within 24 hours of when we receive your order and will get to you within 2 to 3 days. The cost is $7.00 for the first book and $4.00 for each additional book.

**Canadian** shipping rates add 25% to postage total
**Foreign** shipping rates add 50% to the postage total.

All Canadian and foreign orders are shipped book rate, Rush Service is not available

## 100% SATISFACTION GUARANTEE!!!

We value your support. You will receive a full refund as long as the copy of the book you are not happy with is received back by us in reasonable condition. No questions asked, except we would like to know how we failed you. Refunds and credits are given as soon as we receive back the book.

_____Trek: The Lost Years $12.95    ISBN#1-55698-220-8

_____Trek: The Next Generation $14.95    ISBN#1-55698-305-0

_____Trek: Twentyfifth Anniversary Celebration $14.95    ISBN#1-55698-290-9

_____The Making Of The Next Generation $14.95    ISBN#1-55698-219-4

_____The Best Of Enterprise Incidents: The Mag For Star Trek Fans $9.95 ISBN#1-55698-231-3

_____The History Of Trek $14.95    ISBN#1-55698-309-3

_____Trek Fan's Handbook $9.95    ISBN#1-55698-271-2

_____The Trek Crewbook $9.95    ISBN#1-55698-257-7

_____The Man Between The Ears: Star Trek's Leonard Nimoy $14.95    ISBN#1-55698-304-2

_____The Doctor And The Enterprise $9.95    ISBN#1-55698-218-6

_____The Lost In Space Tribute Book $14.95    ISBN#1-55698-226-7

_____The Complete Lost In Space $19.95

_____The Lost In Space Tech Manual $14.95

_____Doctor Who: The Complete Baker Years $19.95    ISBN#1-55698-147-3

_____The Doctor Who Encyclopedia: The Baker Years $19.95  ISBN#1-55698-160-0

_____Doctor Who: The Pertwee Years $19.95    ISBN#1-55698-212-7

_____Number Six: The Prisoner Book $14.95    ISBN#1-55698-158-9

_____Gerry Anderson: Supermarionation $14.95

_____The L.A. Lawbook $14.95    ISBN#1-55698-295-X

_____The Rockford Phile $14.95    ISBN#1-55698-288-7

_____Cheers: Where Everybody Knows Your Name $14.95    ISBN#1-55698-291-7

_____It's A Bird It's A Plane $14.95    ISBN#1-55698-201-1

_____The Green Hornet Book $16.95 Edition

_____How To Draw Art For Comic Books $14.95    ISBN#1-55698-254-2

_____How To Create Animation $14.95    ISBN#1-55698-285-2

_____Rocky & The Films Of Stallone $14.95    ISBN#1-55698-225-9

_____The New Kids Block $9.95    ISBN#1-55698-242-9

_____Monsterland Fearbook $14.95

_____The Unofficial Tale Of Beauty And The Beast $14.95    ISBN#1-55698-261-5

_____The Hollywood Death Book $14.95    ISBN#1-55698-307-7

_____The Addams Family Revealed $14.95    ISBN#1-55698-300-X

_____The Dark Shadows Tribute Book $14.95    ISBN#1-55698-234-8

_____Stephen King & Clive Barker: An Illustrated Guide $14.95 ISBN#1-55698-253-4

_____Stephen King & Clive Barker: Illustrated Guide II $14.95 ISBN#1-55698-310-7

_____The Fab Films Of The Beatles $14.95    ISBN#1-55698-244-5

_____Paul McCartney: 20 Years On His Own $9.95    ISBN#1-55698-263-1

# *For the best in entertainment books!*

---

Couch Potato, Inc.
5715 N. Balsam Road
Las Vegas, Nevada 89130

## TO: